SURVIVAL

SURVIVAL

Poets Speak (while we still can), vol. 5

Edited by John Roche

Beatlick Press
&
Jules' Poetry Playhouse Publications
Albuquerque, NM

Poets Speak (while we still can) is a series of mini-anthologies addressing the current national and planetary crisis.

Series Editor: John Roche
Associate Editor: Jules Nyquist
Art Editor: Denise Weaver Ross

Cover Design: Denise Weaver Ross
Frontispiece Illustration: Jules Nyquist, *Trinity Site Obelisk*
Section I Illustration: Sylvia Ramos Cruz, *Patria o Muerte*
Section II Illustration: Gretchen Schulz, *FUANONYMOUS*
Section III Illustration: John Roche, *Holly Wilson and Pamela Hirst at Bookworks*
Section IV Illustration: Gretchen Schulz, *Building the Cabin, 1956*
Section V Illustration: Dwain Wilder, *Great Sky Spirit*
Section VI Illustration: John Roche, *Resist!*

Special thanks to Beatlick Press publisher Pamela Hirst and Beatlick Press editor Deborah Woodside Coy!

ISBN-13: 978-1722612412
ISBN-10: 172261241X

Printed in the United States of America

All copyrights remain with the authors, artists and photographers

Copyright ©2018 Beatlick Press and Jules' Poetry Playhouse Publications, all rights reserved

Acknowledgments

The following poems have appeared elsewhere:

Sam Abrams' "American Renaissance Criminals" appeared on *Napalm Health Spa/The Museum of American Poetics* (2003), and on *First of the Month: A Website of the Radical Imagination*, Sept. 25, 2016.

H. M. Aragon's "Dark and Light Side of the Moon" was published in a chapbook titled *When Desert Willows Speak* (Lummox Press, 2015).

Gary Brower's "Escaping the End of the World" is the title poem of a collection published by Village Books Press in 2017.

Lauren Camp's "No Matter the Time" first appeared in *Avatar Review* in 2014, and her "Tort of Outrage" appeared in *Construction* in Jan. 2007.

Larry Goodell's "Unwanted" is part of "Comic Invasion," which is in *Nothing to Laugh About: Poems 2015 & 2016* (Beatlick Press, 2018).

Veronica Golos' "Rain Song" is from *Vocabulary of Silence* (Red Hen Press, 2011).

Mark Granier's "Sing, Words" previously appeared in his collection *Fade Street* (Salmon Press, 2010.)

David Landrey's "Consciousness Suite: XXXI" appeared in his book *Consciousness Suite* (Spuyten Duyvil, 2008).

Jane Lipman's "Unsung" won Second Place in the "Honoring Cole Porter" national contest (Humanities theme), 2015.

Ezra Lipschitz's "What Remains" and "A Serious Laughter" appeared in *Apocalypse Soon - The Mostly Unedited Poems of Ezra E. Lipschitz* (edited by Nathan L. Brown).

David Michael Nixon's "Advice From A Volunteer Firefighter" first appeared in *Lake Effect* 6:4, Winter 1992.

Charles Rossiter's "Beware" was previously published in *Back Beat* (Cross Roads Press, 2001; 2nd edition, Fractal Edge Press, 2006).

Elaine G. Schwartz's "The Flautist" was previously published in *The Sunday Poem, Duke City Fix*, Aug. 14, 2016, and in *Malpais Review*, Winter 2011, Placitas, NM.

Joseph Somoza's "Vegetation" appeared in his most recent book, *As Far As I Know* (Cinco Puntos Press, 2015).

F. Richard Thomas's "These Days" appeared in *Cacti Fur*, Jan. 4, 2017.

Denise Weaver Ross's "How to Survive the Space–Time Continuum" appeared in *Poems Underwater* (2013), and her "Heart Transplant" appeared in the chapbook *House of Cards: The House Suit* (2014).

Beverly Zeimer's "Child Dreaming During the Cold War" was published in *Pudding 53* (Spring 2007). This same poem appears in her new chapbook *The Wildness of Flowers*, from Night Ballet Press.

Preface

Survival is volume five of *Poets Speak (while we still can)*, a series of anthologies in response to the national and planetary crisis provoked by the election of 11/8/16. The other volumes are titled *Trumped*, *Hers*, *Water*, and *Walls*.

All profits arising from this series will be donated to the following organizations: The Southwest Women's Law Center, the American Civil Liberties Union, the Southern Poverty Law Center, the National Immigration Law Center, and the Indigenous Environmental Network.

We wish to thank all the poets and artists who are contributing to this project!

Jules Nyquist, *Trinity Site Obelisk*

Contents

I.
3. Denise Weaver Ross, *How to Survive the Space–Time Continuum*
4. David Michael Nixon, *Advice From a Volunteer Firefighter*
5. Margaret Plaganis, *First Aid for Surviving Volcanoes*
7. Denise Weaver Ross, *Heart Transplant*
8. Merimee Moffitt, *Truce*
9. Lydia Andrews, *How to Take Your First Call at the Drop-in Center*
10. Richard Vargas, *a note to the young artists living in these dark days*
11. Jane Sadowsky, *Survival Techniques for Life in America the Great*
12. John Roche, *Joe the Poet's Guide to Surviving Fascism*
13.. Steve Ausherman, *I Have Devised a Plan*
14. David Michael Nixon, *We're All in the Same Swamp*
15. Mary Elizabeth Lang, *How to Escape From Quicksand*
16. Charles Rossiter, *Beware*
18. Mary Dudley, *In These Times*
19. Scott Wiggerman, *You're Not Alone*
20. Nathanael William Stolte, *Wither Worm*
21. Deborah Coy, *Now Is the Time for All Good Men (and Women) to Come to the Aid of Their Country*
22. Sarita Sol González, *Wake Up*
24. Mary Ellen Kelly, *How to Wake Up (after the election)*
26. Larry Goodell, *Que Pasa Picasso?*
28. Sam Abrams, *American Renaissance Criminals*

II.
33. Megan Baldridge, *Minimally Thriving, With a Little Tubing*
35. David Morse, *This Call May Be Monitored*
36. Rich Boucher, *First Rich Corinthians (Chap. 4, Vers. 1)*
38. John Berry, *Dreaming of Rome*
40. Maril Nowak, *It's Really Not My Business*
41. Kitty Jospé, *Words*
42. Kathamann, *Our Predicament*
43. Herb Kauderer, *Stay on the Lookout*
44. Margaret Randall, *Love Is Easier Than Hate*
45. Lauren Camp, *Tort of Outrage*
46. Elise Stuart, *Infrasound*
47. Steven Deridder, *Opinion Spindle*
48. Alice Lee, *Hitler's Germany*
50. Patricia Roth Schwartz, *Resistance (France 1940-44)*
51. Karla Linn Merrifield, *Cherita Triptyck: Good Trumps Evil*
52. Michael C. Ford, *Appointment in Pakistan*

53. John Landry, *American Odyssey*
54. Kenneth P. Gurney, *Protest*
55. Kathamann, *Amen*
56. Mari Simbaña, *Cuttings*
58. Mari Simbaña, *I eat my country, in hopes of remembering*
59. Danielle Taana Smith, *Sole Survivors*
60. Chad Parenteau, *First Attack*
61. Beverly Zeimer, *Child Dreaming During the Cold War*
62. Gayle Lauradunn, *United States History*
64. Arthur O. DuBois, *To Dust You Shall Return*
65. Tony Brown, *Predators*
67. Kenneth P. Gurney, *Run, Friend, Run!*
68. Joanne Bodin, *Pontoon Politics*
69. Mary Strong Jackson, *Surviving 45*
70. Ceinwen Haydon, *Pandemonium's New Dawn*
71. Vincent F. A. Golphin, *Steel Blues (for Youngstown, Ohio)*
73. Nicolas Eckerson, *To the unchanged city structures*
75. Summer Brenner, *Laid Off on Franklin Street*
77. Kitty Jospé, *Wait—it's not too late*
78. Mary Oertel–Kirschner, *Secret Message*
79. G. E. Schwartz, *Knowing Others Have*
80. F. Richard Thomas, *These Days*
81. Jared Smith, *Early November in an Election Year*
82. Mark W. Ó Brien, *Incubus*
84. David Morse, *Credo for Fierce Times*
85. Steven Deridder, *Forms in the Aftermath*
86. Stewart S. Warren, *Rolling Through*

III.
89. Holly Wilson, *Didn't' Die Today*
91. Lauren Camp, *No Matter the Time*
92. Nicolas Eckerson, *Survival of the Self*
93. Gayle Lauradunn, *Ease*
94. Catherine Iselin, *A Lifetime of Toiling*
95. Georgia Santa Maria, *Hospital*
96. Kevin Higgins, *In the White Man's Clinic*
97. Freya Manfred, *Many Things Frighten Me*
98. Sheryl Guterl, *Verge*
99. Stephen Ellis, *I Confess*
103. Jesse Ehrenberg, *Here There Be Monsters*
105. Marc Schillace, *Leaving*
106. John Roche, *Joe on the Border*
107. Martin Willitts, Jr., *Sonnet: The Lessons I've Learned So Far; Turns Out, There's More to Learn*

108. Joseph Somoza, *Vegetation*
110. Roslye Ultan, *The Bells Began to Ring*
111. John Landry, *Lesson in Detachment*
112. Dwain Wilder, *Tap Tap*
113. Dick Bakken, *Planning for What You Don't Want to Happen*
114. Martin Willitts, Jr., *Sonnet: Rain Followed Me Home*
115. Bill Nevins, *wings*
116. Manuel Gonzalez, *Grief, Guilt, Gratitude*
117. Larry Schulte, *Friends for Life*
119. Mark Fleisher, *On the Edge*
120. Scott Wiggerman, *Twilight Time*
121. Michele Brown, *Survival*
123. Lawrence Welsh, *The Man from AA*
124. Declan Quinn, *Cheer Up!*
125. Merimee Moffitt, *we do what we can*
126. Joanne S. Bodin, *In a Colorless World*
127. Mark Granier, *Sing, Words*
128. Ezra Lipschitz, *What Remains*
130. Declan Quinn, *Closer*
131. Kate Bremer, *Five Points of Connection*
132. Kate Bremer, *Prayer Blanket*
133. G.E. Schwartz, *Balm*
134. Mary McGinnis, *Yes, Little Mind*
135. Margaret Randall, *Younger Than That Now*
136. Maril Nowak, *Switching Off the News to Observe Crocus*
137. Wendy Heath, *Deer*
138. Mary Dudley, *The Mountains Watch*
139. Janet Eigner, *Motherhood in the Mountain Mahogany*
140. Linda Yen, *The Second That Flew By*
142. Gretchen Schulz, *Tornado People*
143. Mina Hatami, *The I*
145. H. M. Aragon, *The Dark and Light Side of the Moon*
147. Colleen Powderly, *By Dark Light*
148. Elaine G. Schwartz, *The Flautist*
149. Jane Lipman, *Unsung*
150. Jennifer Maloney, *Detained*
153. Karla Linn Merrifield, *Breaking Silence*
154. Janet Ruth, *Song for Us Who Are Working Our Way Through*
156. Ray Johnson, *Let Us*
157. Kate Marco, *subversive*
158. Lauren McLean Ayer, *Lullaby*
159. Lyn Lifshin, *The Geranium*
160. Alexis Rhone Fancher, *Tonight We Will Blossom for One Night Only*
161. Robbie Sugg, *Some Edens*

IV.
163. Demetria Martinez, *Inauguration Day, 2017*
164. Bill Nevins, *Cutting It So Close*
165. Deborah Coy, *Half-Life of a Fruitcake*
166. Patricia Roth Schwartz, *Carol, Baking Bread*
167. Mary McGinnis, *Stay, Time*
168. Loren Niemi, *Thursday Morning*
169. Steve Tills, *Occasionally Poems*
170. Alecia Lutrario, *An Ode to the Initials Carved into the Bridge*
171. William Heyen, *Sustenance*
172. William Heyen, *Achilles*
173. Fred Whitehead, *Salvage*
174. David Landrey, *Consciousness Suite XXXI*
175. Orin Domenico, *Among the Daily Dirt*
177. Ed Sanders, *On the Way to Allen Ginsberg's 92nd Birthday Celebration at the Howl Gallery on E. 1st*
179. Jules Nyquist, *How to Send a Petroglyph into the Future*
180. Freya Manfred, *On Carpinteria Beach*
181. Renny Golden, *Chief Shabonna's Vision*
182. Ray Johnson, *Sweet Old Navaho*
183. Sylvia Ramos Cruz, *At the Precipice*
184. John Roche, *Echoing*

V.
187. Dwain Wilder, *Great Sky Spirit*
188. Larry Goodell, *Unwanted*
189. Jared Smith, *The Storm Upon Us*
190. Lauren McLean Ayer, *How to Survive the Flood*
191. Teresa E. Gallion, *Mother*
192. Ezra Lipschitz, *A Serious Laughter*
193. Carlton Holte, *Banjaxed*
194. Michael Peters, *ecological josef albers affordable-care-act light event #19*
195. Leah Zazulyer, *Climate Change*
196. Janet Ruth, *Supposition for a Different Age*
198. Stewart S. Warren, *Freed to Feed Our Young*

VI.
201. Robbie Sugg, *Second Chance*
202. Tina Carlson, *Sorrow and Awe*
203. Veronica Golos, *Inverse: A Ghazal*
204. Mary Strong Jackson, *The Mappist*
205. Janet Eigner, *Code Talkers*
206. Pamela Williams, *Even the Engineer Bots from Ghana*
207. Robert E. McDonough, *Timothy Caughman in California*

208. Alecia Lutrario, *Girl Made of Hazards*
209. Gary Brower, *Escaping the End of the World*
212. Craig Czury, *Wind Hurling Stones*
213. Craig Czury, *Above the Back Alley*
214. Georgia Santa Maria, *Arizona Dogs*
215. Herb Kauderer, *Surviving Low Tide*
216. Dianne Borsenik, *Tides*
217. Martha Deed, *After Whitman*
218. Colleen Powderly, *What Would Walt Whitman Do?*
219. Veronica Golos, *Rain Song*
220. Mark Granier, *The Whew*
221. Martha Treichler, *Survival*

Addenda
222. Bios
240. Publishers' Page

Another World Is Possible!

Si, se puede!

I.

Sylvia Ramos Cruz, *Patria o Muerte*

Denise Weaver Ross

How to Survive the Space–Time Continuum

Live in negative space,
walk along the edge of lines,
disappear under wave tops,
surf over sine and cosign.

Skim buoyantly over reefs,
scrape belly and back,
let the sand and the undertow
pull, retract, push, recede.

Dive to the sea floor,
dance with extremophiles,
suck life from hydrothermal vents.
7,000 feet under the sea.

Rocket to a new world,
thrive a moment at 750 degrees,
then dying, build new life
from the molecular level.

Divide, subtract, multiply,
breathe between nanoseconds.

David Michael Nixon

Advice From a Volunteer Firefighter

Do not always turn away,
but sometimes hold your face
to the fire; eyebrows and lashes
may singe off, the skin redden
and peel, but the brain, the nerves
will shake and tremble
until the phantoms of flames
move in your synapses
and you can fight fire
with its image,
as the training film on napalm
exploded in my guts,
leaving my will for war white ash.

Margaret Plaganis

First Aid for Surviving Volcanoes

When Mount St. Helens' volcano erupted in Washington state,
it spewed clouds of ash and pumice for days. I monitored
its monstrous cloud-plumes blooming like nuclear events
outside my kitchen window, and prayed prevailing winds would
keep the deadly air away from me, seventy miles south in Oregon City.

Though it happened long ago, I've kept this volcano-first-aid advice
from a survivor lived to walk off the mountain after it exploded.

FIRST, BEFORE you face AWAY from the on-coming cloud,
LOOK WHERE YOU ARE!
RUN! But don't run the all the way!
You'll breathe too deep and fast when the cloud hits!
COVER your nose and mouth at least!
COVER your eyes and face!
Put a shirt, jacket, pants or empty backpack OVER YOUR HEAD.
If there's time, douse a cloth or clothing with coffee,
tea, water or urine, and COVER YOUR NOSE AND MOUTH!

REMEMBER THE DIRECTION YOU ARE FACING
BECAUSE EVERYTHING AFTER THE CLOUD
WILL LOOK BLACK & GREY.
Everything will look the same.
NO ground. NO background.
NO sky. NO sun.

As the cloud arrives,
sit down behind anything –
some brush - a rock, a tree.
CLOSE YOUR EYES FAST.
PROTECT YOUR SIGHT
SO YOU CAN WALK OUT LATER.
(It might be as black as night
if you open them anyway.)
Remain motionless! Do not talk!

When you think the winds
have stopped or things might be
clear or settled, DO NOT STAND UP!
There MIGHT be LIGHTNING!

WET A NEW CLOTH IF YOU HAVE ONE –
Replace the first! The air is NOT breathable!
It will be a strange FOG of miniscule ash and dust
particles that will linger in the air for a very long time!

Denise Weaver Ross

Heart Transplant

You must prepare yourself
for the operation. This may take
a long time, and there is no guarantee
that a donor heart will be found.

Abstinence, therapy, and meditation
are recommended; avoid drugs and
an excess of alcohol, which will only
make your heart's problems worse.

If you find a compatible donor heart,
cut in between your ribs, forcing
your ribcage open, leaving your
damaged heart exposed but beating.

Connect your circulatory system
to the heart-lung machine; breathe.
Stop your heart.

Slice open the protective pericardium
and remove your heart, leaving only
the back part of your left atrium.
Trim and reshape the donor heart;
fit the new heart into what remains.

With luck, your donor heart
will start beating. Disconnect
the machine; remember to breathe.

Give yourself time to recover;
take your anti-rejection medication.

You have survived, taken a risk,
been given a gift. Choose joy.

Parts of the poem are "found" and quoted directly from the University of California's "Patient's Guide to Heart Transplant Surgery."

Merimee Moffitt

Truce

Overall, be kind. Don't tell me
you don't know what kindness is.
German and British soldiers lay down weapons
took up cigars, played cards and soccer
Some had whiskey, all had orders for a truce
a Christmas truce in 1914,
next day, resumed the business of war
the job they were paid for.

Kindness was in that deal, relief, good memories.
In Vietnam, the troops took up heroin
and most, upon return, could lay it down.
Some healed themselves in the warmth of
Grandma's allowances or a wife's desire.

I lay my judgments down, tonight, my fear, my worry
and bursts of anger, like laying my comb back into the
cosmetic bag. Like putting away the weight of the world
allowing my neck and shoulders to relax, my lungs
to breathe and to enjoy the flame of my own life.

It is human to remember and forget in endless cycles.
Oh it is a kindness to myself to remember that I
control so little, and all that I can control is myself.
If it's a kindness to bite my tongue, so be it.
If it's a kindness to listen, then let it happen. If my mouth
has a kindness to share, then open it. Do no harm.

We are all doctors in the arena of addiction. Kindness is the
only tool, the only medication, the only recommended
intervention.

Lydia Andrews

How to Take Your First Call at the Crisis Center

1. Arrange pen and paper. Write your alias where you can see it, to clothe yourself in this clumsy new identity.
2. Breathe. Breathe as if the impending ring will split the universe, but you won't mind.
3. Lift the receiver, with your hand shaking, as if this action will open a hole in the floor, and you will fall through into a dream that isn't yours. You will do this for a long time. Eventually, it will feel easy. At least as easy as reaching for anything will ever be.
4. Hear the click, followed by the silence. Ask yourself how your voice failed, like a sieve, to contain that moment.
5. Hear six more clicks, six more silences.
6. Hear voice. Absorb it as if it is the first human voice you have ever heard.
7. Ask, "What's on your mind?" and make sure that every breath says, "I'm here, I'm here," continual respiration of closeness, saying, "I'm so glad you are here too."
8. Listen.

Richard Vargas

a note to the young artists living in these dark days

go paint a picture in the rain
and watch the colors run or
write a poem while getting drunk
and listen to the random noise
of empty bottles breaking in the street
pick up a drum and beat it mad
as you dance naked in the backyard
under a suburban moon or drive
to the beach and sing jazz
to the stars hanging in a black
ink sky while wearing discarded
rags found in the trash bins
of local thrift stores or get
arrested for carving your visions
into the walls of public restrooms
know that the difference
between a dollar bill and
a sheet of toilet paper
is the green ink
close your eyes and
jump off the cliff
art will catch you
it always does

Jane Sadowsky

Survival Techniques for Life in America the Great

1. Invent your own alternate facts. Behave as if they are universally accepted as truth. Act shocked when someone fails to recognize them as real.

2. Tell your boss that you don't need to attend the ethics in-service, because ethics is so the-day-before-the-inauguration.

3. Find an alt-right cemetery. File the swastikas off the tombstones.

4. Learn to speak Russian.

5. Start raising pileated woodpeckers. Turn them loose on the border wall.

6. Recycle your glass bottles. Fill them with messages like "He doesn't speak for us!" Sign them "the American People." Stand on the beach at dawn and set them free.

7. Petition Canada to annex your town. Learn to say "eh" and "tuque." Call Tim Horton's "Timmy's." Learn curling. Just remember, their version of the "loonie" is a coin (not a head of state).

8. Count your supporters in the millions. Even the three who just saw you eat breakfast at Timmy's.

9. Put up "bear-icades." Protect the environment from the EPA.

10. Fly your American flag backwards, sideways or upside down -- express your feelings on the latest tweet.

11. Turn the pileated woodpeckers loose on the EPA.

12. Try to find the worm hole we fell through on November 8th and work to send us back.

13. Run down the street yelling, "We've hit an iceberg! The ship is going down!"

14. Place ads in the newspaper: "Help wanted: The Doctor and his sonic screwdriver. Someone in power has a screw loose."

John Roche

Joe the Poet's Guide to Surviving Fascism

1. Know who yr true friends are
2. Live near the tracks and keep yr suitcase packed
3. Keep yr passport current
4. Helps to know some folks with a farm or cabin where you could hide out
5. As Woody said, don't expect a handout from the rich, but the poor will share what little they have
6. Keep a sense of humor, even if it's gallows humor
7. Keep yr guitar tuned
8. Keep on writing, but be careful how you share
9. Personal survival is important, but not the most important
10. Remember, you contain multitudes and "me" belongs to "we"

Steve Ausherman

I Have Devised a Plan

Here is how we will do this. Here is how we will endure.

We will not buy survival gear: cans of beans, gas masks, propane, knives.
We will not buy guns or gold. We will not damage synagogues.
We will not look away. We will not build bombs. We will not cry.
We will seek out the news: blogs and newspapers, radio programs and
 television.
We will seek out different ideas: Muslim or Christian or atheist,
 Fox News or CNN.
We will get a library card and we will use it. We will stroll and we will
 ride bikes.
We will talk to our family and friends. We will talk to our enemies.
We will talk to our neighbors. We will talk to postmen and cops.
We will talk to the coworkers we love. We will talk to the coworkers
 we hate.
We will talk to coffee baristas and truck stop waitresses. We will slow
 down.

Here is how we will survive. Here is how we straighten our spines.

We will call our state representatives. We will show up to political
 rallies.
We will be respectful when we talk to politicians. We will speak
 our truth.
We will speak truth to power. We will not vandalize or shout down
 others.
We will have a cup of coffee. We will walk our dogs. We will
 pet our cats.
We will call our mothers. We will forgive our fathers. We will be
 sisters again.
We will tell those who are close to us how much we love them before
 it is too late.
We will stay strong. We will act in ways that our future selves will be
 proud of.
We will open our arms. We will raise our fists. We will open our minds.
We will see ourselves in others. We will hope that others see themselves
 in us.
We will write our names into the book of time. We will endure. We will
 breathe.

David Michael Nixon

We're All in the Same Swamp

Next time you want to shout
names or curses at someone, picture
that person slowly trying to pull out
of quicksand, hand by hand, on a thin vine.

This is where we all are, even if
we can't see it very often.

Open your eyes and reach out.
If we all form a line
to pull toward a firmly rooted tree,
we may hold out a while longer,
before the quicksand sucks us down.

Mary Elizabeth Lang

How to Escape from Quicksand

Let's say you are hiking up a tributary of the Quinnipiac with a partner you just met, a guy named Joe whose physical strength and endurance—never mind his politics and philosophy—you know nothing about. The stream banks are steep and thick with vegetation, and you are finally forced to walk in the stream itself, with all the grace of a moose. Suddenly you come around a bend, and a flock of mallards takes off, serenely skimming the tops of the cattails. And it takes the breath out of both of you.

But seconds later, even before you can begin breathing again, the stream bed falls away and you are both in quicksand up to your waists. Each time one of you extricates a leg, the mud makes a sucking sound and sends up foul-smelling bubbles, then pulls the leg back in. You remember seeing a paperback book last week in the bookstore. The yellow cover promised, among other things, "Learn How to Escape from Quicksand." But you don't remember if you bought the book. If you did, it lies unread on your coffee table.

Let's say that Joe figures out a way to swim on his back like a loon, and he lets you hold his legs until you reach shore. And suppose he then lets you lead him up the bank, both of you crawling through prickly wild raspberries, and in spite of the tension, he stops to savor a few. Now you know everything about Joe that you need to. And you know something else. When you ask the landscape to open up its secrets, you allow it to swallow you whole.

Charles Rossiter

Beware

We who have kept our eyes open
are the last indigenous people of the 21st Century.
Regardless of Afro-Euro-Latino-Asian-Indio
grandmothers, we are together in this
because we are together endangered.   Beware.

. . .of smiling corporations bearing gifts.
Make no mistake, Starbucks is our Cortez
Bordello's Books and music is our Custer
Big Brother's got 99 channels and rising
Wal-Mart comes bearing diseases many
are not immune against. Their parking lots
and paychecks are contaminated and spread
the infection. If you don't believe it,
look around. Small town America is sick
and dying, withered from a lethal dose.   Beware.

People once thought you could not sell
the land because it belongs to everyone
and the Great Spirit, but the land got sold
to those who knew they could buy it
with tricks and mind-numbing gifts and then
they fenced it so it belonged to no one.
They do the same thing with your mind.   Beware.

There are those who believe they are free
but their overstuffed asses are chained
by PizzaHut, Citibank, Microsoft
DunkinDonuts chains to tv armchairs,
decapitation, hacksawgangrape movie houses
machine gun computer games, sick packs
of lite beer and snack bowls of empty
chemicals with names you can't pronounce.   Beware.

We must act now. Pull the plug and vote
with our folded wallets and watch their
bottom lines shrivel in a language they understand--
a ju-jitsu of the dollar as simple as turning off
the tv set

and astounding the Nielsen man when he
picks up the rating box and sees that it reads
"zero."

It's simple as grown-ups talking to kids
simple as a good book and homemade bread
simple as midnight skinny dips filled with wet kisses
simple as not consorting with the enemy
simple as a trail hike.

All over the world, we are everywhere
black, white, red, yellow and brown
all over the world, they are everywhere
black, white, red, yellow and brown.   Beware.
It's not the color or the cut of the clothes
it's the consciousness.

It's us against them
and we
        are our only hope.

Mary Dudley

In These Times

> —*trumpery: adj: showy but worthless*
> *noun: attractive articles of little value or use*

I
To cope in the time of trumpery:
Strive to avoid hysteria.
Cull headlines ruthlessly.
Free your mind of nonsense.

Strive to conquer anxiety and fear.
Defuse confusion; ignore most of what you hear.

If you like to run, run.
If you prefer to walk, then walk
Make time to meet to laugh.
Make time to meet to talk.

Stand with those who need you by their side.
Steer clear of those whose ways you can't abide.

Sit in silence. Then sit some more.
Avoid what makes your spirit seethe.

Sit in silence. Then sit some more.
And breathe. Breathe. And breathe.

II
To make it through the new regime
adopt the cranes' survival strategy:
Rotate the role of sentry
allowing each a period of peace
in which to simply graze
while others maintain vigilance.

Scott Wiggerman

You're Not Alone

—a golden shovel including a Dickinson last line (#926)

We've no more use for patience.
We're tired of slogans and "Blessed is."
For too long, evening news has been the
hour of tears and turmoil, the smile's
absence, an exercise in emotional exertion.

The future doesn't come without effort. Time to push through
useless complaisance. Time to force the
struggle, our minds quaking, our hearts quivering.

Nathanael William Stolte

Wither Worm

much
like
rain
brings
worms
out
from
the
safety
of
wet
soil
onto
black-
top
&
side-
walks—
this
admin-
istra-
tion
is
bring-
ing
the
vill-
ains
out—
&
when
the
sun
comes
out—
worms
wi-
ther
in
its
light

Deborah Coy

Now is the Time for all Good Men (and Women)
to Come to the Aid of Their Country

Good men, praise your mothers
and pet your pets and
love your soul to save it.
But when Washington gropes,
grope back!
When our leaders love money,
love earth more.
When they dismantle,
put on the mantle of a prophet.

But it is not yet the time
to tell them,
"I told you so."
There is no profit in that.
Wait till the old starve,
when unwanted babies
are hung from coat hangers,
when love is no longer legal,
when little children
work for their own food,
when our lands burn,
when our waters rage,
when the planet shakes
to shake us off.
Wait until our rivers run with
the blood of the earth.
Wait until you huddle
in smog and dark.

Then you can tell them,
"I told you so."

But now it is time to fight.
It is time to say, "NO!"

Sarita Sol González

Wake up

Wake up
4:30 am
I awake to the sound of my alarm blaring in my ear
I eat, wash up, get my clothes on and leave for school Wake up
When I get there
Everything is normal
We hang out
Go to class
Fire alarm
But just a drill
Have lunch
Another class
And finally the school day is almost done
Wake up
2:21 pm
Wait
The fire alarm
Going off again?
I hear gunshots...
The noise sounds like my alarm to Wake Up
The school goes into a lockdown WAKE UP
It's so loud
I'm afraid that he will hear me breath After 6 minutes of shooting
I hear silence
Where should I go
I cant breathe, I can't tell the difference between the gunshots and my pounding heart
Will I make it out?
Questions run thru my mind
How many are gone
What will happen to their families
I'm praying that I don't scream out my broken sanity WAKE UP
We all flee
WAKE UP
Where's the shooter
WAKE UP
WAKE UP
Wake up to the pain
Wake up to the carnage

I have lost my innocence
along with so many others
My dreams are corrupted
And have now turned into nightmares
Wake up parents
Your children need to have your support
To make schools what they are meant to be
A place of learning
You need to stand with us
Relate to us
Don't hold us back from making change
Wake up Republicans and Democrats
Protect the youth you BOTH claim to care about What is more important to you?
Your party
Or your children
Wake up white house
Hold yourself to your word
 Because without your word You are nothing
WAKE UP WORLD Because now
Some of our peers can't and will never again
Wake up
My generation has awoken
We are the ones that have been forced to speak out Because we have the most to lose
Look at what we have done
We have created a movement
That has no sign of stopping
With the message that enough is enough
We are calling BS
We are saying never again
We are making a stand for future generations Our generation is WOKE
So quit hitting your snooze button
WAKE UP!!!

Mary Ellen Kelly

How to Wake Up (after the election)

Set your alarm on a soft ring
Try ocean sounds
or Tibetan bowls

Set it for as late as you can
because you're not sleeping well
with all those cold shivers
deep in the bone

After you reach over and push the snooze button
stay in bed for a very long time
It'll be easier that way

When you hear the second alarm
you'll know there's no turning back
Do it. Stand up, breathe, walk, look in the mirror
Don't be shocked if you look the same as yesterday

Get dressed in your best
Brushy brush everything that needs it
These are lipstick days. Do it
Final face check

Avoid turning on the radio until after breakfast
Just eat. Granola will do
It's easy
which is good because you haven't begun
to think. Not yet. Hold off if you can

Pat your animals, watch the birds at the feeder
Marvel at the wonder of morning light
Look through the binoculars for signs of wild turkey
Hope for mystery moose

Now, turn on the news
He's on the radio. He's going to be there
for a long time. Act like you don't care
Pretend he can see you ignoring him

Steal the word from him
Hold it in your arms: "Immigrant"
He can't have it

Carry the word with you all day
When you're sure he's not watching
run to the shore
to the sandy beach and keep running

Feel the heart of the wind
Remember the word
Fly it like a kite, the string in your hand,
Watch it hover and loop
Hear the laughter
Open your palm

Larry Goodell

Qué Pasa Picasso?

Ugly vanity
ugliness tainted with
poison inside –
one accolade after another
can't sustain
the bric-a-brac ego
based on
everything gone wrong –
emollients become
emoluments.

Qué pasa Picasso?
Where has true greatness gone
and we're left with
a leader of fine filth
total devastation
of good
a lying excuse for
humanity
unhumaned –
sad trace of flesh
getting everything wrong
and proving it
as the evil cohorts
come out of the closet,
the gangs of uncivil idiots
multiply under the vermin watch
of their leader.

If beauty is to survive
every freed discipline
of creativity must take the spotlight,
can only put out art
before art is put out,
bring out every play poem painting
performance song ensemble
band orchestra instrument jazz
hip hop to sustained opera
singing at its heart level,
the intense comic satiric

art forms of words
and all music at high
determined outflow
in the most beautiful
song of survival ever to exist.

We are creating an exit to madness
a restoration of the best of our
revolutionary drama –
qué pasa Picasso,
I see you everywhere
we are all reasserting
our improvised strength
to topple the most pathetic
bitch of our time
the effete poophead
of our would-be destruction.

Qué pasa Picasso?
Everywhere create ourselves
out of this madness.

Sam Abrams

American Renaissance Criminals

let it be remembered that America's literary pantheon
is full of nuts and felons
crazy Emily won't come down
drug fiend Poe queer Whitman
even triple-barreled Harvard men

Ralph
Waldo
Emerson

Henry
David
Thoreau

felonious fellows

both in that riotous mob
impeded federal authorities
doing their lawful duty
trying to take into custody
Frank Sanborn Concord schoolmaster
of the notorious Secret Six
who financed John Brown's
attack on a federal arsenal
Secret Sixer got away

and if the feds had managed
to jail Frank Sanborn
Whitman was ready
part of an armed gang
conspirators
ready to spring him

when one of John Brown's Liberators escaped
Frank Merrian
wanted on the run he came
to Samuel Gridley Howe Secret Sixer
Sam lost his nerve
turned hin from his door

Sam Howe good man,
comrade of Byron
fought to free Greece
that day
his nerve broke

George Luther Stearns Secret Sixer
good man staunch abolitionist
Merriam came to him
he copped out too
freaked out
no help

but when Frank finally made it to Concord
where that shot heard round the world
echoes yet in some ears

schoolmaster Sanborn
hid him
super-sage Emerson
loaned horse and shay
eccentric Henry
drove Frank to the station

quickly, efficiently, criminally
no hesitating, no doubt
literary gods
help one of the most wanted men in the USA
to get safe away to Canada

very serious
very serious crime
very serious criminals
Henry and Ralph Waldo

very effective criminals

poets know how
know how when what who
to disobey

poets with outlaw instincts
outlaw reactions reflexes

could be all true poets outlaws?

even Harvard men?

Thomas Wentworth Higginson
Brahmin of the Brahmins
mentor to Emily Dickinson
attacked a jailer with a sword
trying to free
enslaved Anthony Burns

I speak not of living poets
but in the previous generation
the leaders of the schools
Robert Lowell first among the genteel
adorned with many prizes
Alan Ginsberg
adored and scorned
first among the roughnecks

both served jail time
for crimes of conscience

and who helped Tom Paine
hunted by the British authorities
hid him in his house
till he could get out of the country

it was William Blake
the poet friend of angels
and of revolutionaries

so bless them all
Oh Great Muse Co-Conspirator
honor the outlaw poets
now and forever

amen

II.

Gretchen Schulz, FUANONYMOUS

Megan Baldrige

Minimally Thriving, With a Little Tubing

In case I don't survive
the Trump years,
remember to tell Barak and Michelle
and the POTUS dogs,
Bo and Sunny,
that I loved them very much.

In case, I lose consciousness
on Inauguration Day,
don't revive me
until 2020,
then don't share
anything that happened.

Should Hillary, Mario or Ted
run again,
minimally hydrate me, but
respect my wish to be a long-term amnesiac.
Leave me attached to tubes, strapped in,
comatose for four more years.

In case I cannot stomach
the bile bubbling through my veins,
in case my TrumpCare card
cannot cure my case of outrage,
you have my permission to fly me
to any country with a thoughtful president.

In case I am seized by
an overactive gall (his or mine)
my dear friends:
do not let me buy firearms
with no background check,
over the internet from my crazy neighbor.

Should you find me crazed,
clinging in my closet to tarnished truths,
remove my television and radio,

let me wander my neighborhood
with a rechargeable flashlight,
telling my truths,
Uttering words like "unprecedented"
just like a real newscaster does.

And, shake me awake,
when four years
is up.

David Morse

This Call May Be Monitored

Your call is important to us.
Due to unusually high volume,
your inquiry will be answered
by the next available human
in the order it was received.
This call may be monitored
in order to insure quality.
To download the second stanza
of this poem, check
I agree, I agree, I agree.

Please use care
in opening the overhead bins,
as contents may have shifted
since the 2016 election.
Sorry, this password's no good tonight.
You lose your favorite pet,
your mother's maiden name.
You must choose a new persona,
lose your virtual friends,
go before a robot judge
and plea for amnesty.

Rich Boucher

First Rich Corinthians (Chap.4, Vers.1)

Supposedly someone once said that
insanity is doing the same thing over and over again
and expecting different results or expecting the Spanish Inquisition
I can't remember which at this moment
and I'm told that evidently Einstein was the person who said that
but I think there's plenty of reason to doubt whether or not Einstein
even *existed*
since we're now living in the Seventh Dimension
which is the dimension comprised of cosmic particles, sentient tweets and alternative facts
and in this brand new and quite grand dimension
we are all held for ransomware
while the ubiquitous and militarized police
walk back to their cruisers to see if they can get authorization
and hydroplaning means to slide uncontrollably on the wet surface of a road
and I'm sliding uncontrollably on the surface of *the 24-hour news cycle*
and while a gargoyle is defined as
a grotesque carved human or animal face or figure,
projecting from the gutter of a building and typically acting as a spout
to carry water clear of a wall I am defined as
someone who is going to insanely continue to hope for a better day
which might mean that I need to get my head examined or unpacked
but that might just be me being ableist against myself
because I've evidently contracted United-States-flavored Stockholm Syndrome
and a melodrama
a melodrama
a melodrama
a melodrama
is *not* defined as *a mellow dream,*
is defined as *a sensational dramatic piece*
with exaggerated characters and exciting events
intended to appeal to the emotions
but I've only got so many emotions left to spare:
this is 2017
this is two-thousand-and-seventeen
this is the year of our overlord two-thousand-and-seventeen
and one definition of bondage is
the sexual practice that involves *the tying up or restraining of one partner*
and another definition of bondage is the state of *being someone else's slave*
and if the President is going to continue fucking us
while *coup d'etat'ing* us into a corner store

can we all at least ask for ball-gags to drown out our screams
and a theater is defined as
a building or outdoor area in which plays and other dramatic performances are given
and every day we look around
and find that all the store fronts and school fronts
are just clapboard facades *with nothing behind them*
and I regret to inform you that this poem
is not allowing cameras in the room today
and you are not allowed to report on the things announced in this poem
and you are no longer permitted to take pictures of this poem
and this poem will only be available for a few minutes behind the bushes
at 1600 Pennsylvania Ave
and no recording devices are going to be allowed
and any questions about why this is happening will not be allowed
and subjugation is defined as
the action of bringing someone or something under domination or control
and some nights I wake up
to find Sean Spicer kneeling down beside my bed
his face only inches from mine
and he says *you better not say anything*
and cotton candy is defined as
a mass of fluffy spun sugar, *usually pink or white*, wrapped around a stick or a paper cone
and I wish I *was* a mass of fluffy and spun sugar
instead of this mass of frustrated and confused human skin and blood cells
wondering where the hell all my votes went
and sometimes I feel *unusually pink and white*
and even though I do not believe in God
I'm told that God doesn't take offense to that
which is a good thing, a happy accident, a boon and a feather
because I'm feeling the need to open up The Book of Gibberish
and turn to Chapter Four, Verse One of *First Rich Corinthians;*
I'm feeling the need to holler and imprecate
until the all that lightning in the clouds tonight
stitches together some words that maybe I can live by
until such time as I've got nothing more to worry about.

John Berry

Dreaming of Rome

And then a great host
Came together—

Jung and Oak, Tubman and Water,
Twain and Elephant, Basho and Whale
Gandhi and Sparrow, Boxwood, Cicada, O'Keeffe.

And they laid a great canvas over Rome;
Rome and all of its crumbling temples.

And in the ways which suited them best
They swam or flooded, hopped or walked
Or rolled to its center

And began to powder
The madness of its sprawling bones,

The dust of it all
In great white clouds escaping the edges,

Laying upon the rivers surface
Like a sleeping child,

Drifting out to sea,
Its Potomac mother losing her name
In the froth of the ocean.

And when Rome was perfectly flat
Except for the slightest of curves
Of the Earth

They pulled the canvas away, folding it up
And laying it over the elephant's back
Like a saddle,

All heading north to Babylon,
Waterlogged, struggling under its weight
To remain a Manhattan island.

And out of the dust of Rome

The pigeons flew and the naked Senators,
Stripped of their glorious tunics

Stood in silent wonder
Watching the sands disappear

Down the hourglass hole
Where a white house had been.

Maril Nowak

It's Really Not My Business

My neighbor's in the gun shop buying ammo for his Uzi. And I
really don't know why the thought of that upsets me so.

They say Arctic ice is melting up where Exxon will be drilling,
and the climate change is killing polar bears. Now, that upsets me.
They are cuter than the dickens on the Christmas cards I send out
with a little bit of glitter, just a bit of sparkle that makes it extra special.

With the price of oil dropping, my baby brother traded in his Prius for a
Ford F-150 with a Supercab and 4 x 4. I say that's his problem when
he's at the intersection, you know, waiting for a green light as it sits
there sucking gas? I sure wouldn't want his payments, but no skin off
my nose.

Now my little grandkids warn me not to buy those cards with glitter.
They say some Ranger named Rick told them glitter washes into
waterways and oceans where the fishes fill their bellies
because they think it's fish food, after which they starve to death.
I wonder if that Ranger has been watching too much fake news.

Again, my neighbor's coming from the gun shop where he's bought
another Uzi, and I don't know why the thought of that should bother
me so much. I just hope it's got a gun lock. Y'know, he has little
grandkids. But it's really not my business, is it.

Kitty Jospé

Words

> *Human perception is not a direct consequence of reality,*
> *but rather an act of imagination*—Faraday

He says one thing and she counters
it's just that
which means she doesn't believe him.
And the eyewitness fills in the gap
and the judge draws conclusions.

And the Bacon scholar loosely quotes
understanding has a magnet, so
if one thing has appeared as evidence
to confirm an opinion, it will tap
into the comprehension so no matter
what is contrary will not be noticed
and the opinion unshaken.

and someone else quotes the butterfly effect

And truth, no matter which version,
is up for grabs.

So just say "*no*"
if you are in pain. Just say
not my business that fire and fury
are reinstated to activate a cold war.
You're at odds with the times,
and there's nothing you can do about it.
Nothing slashes a madman's budget.

So, what if we budget madmen,
slash nothing,
add nothing to the odds
to the times, the cold war
reinstated to activate fire and fury,
business, just not mine.
In pain? No? Just say so.

Kathamann

Our Predicament

I'm afraid of the mentality
of half of this country. I
don't know how to show them
what they can't see. I want to
warn them:

>	DANGER
>	DANGER
>	DANGER

They are too busy to read the
writing on the wall.
They will not change.
They don't want to change.
They don't know how to change.

They are my siblings. I have to
learn to embrace them and maybe
we can change together.

Herb Kauderer

Stay on the Lookout

for the zealot,
the unrepentant conservative
    who cannot see greatness
    in kindness and civility
sees only the faux greatness
    of bullying & pomposity
believes freedom to hurt
    & be hurt
    will toughen us up
sees 1950s America as an ideal
    which it might have been
    if you were a white
    male professional.
Assume all suspects
to be ideologically armed
and dangerous to any
dissenting viewpoint.
Approach with caution,
kindness, patience,
and unwavering resolve.
Do not be afraid to call
for backup.

Margaret Randall

Love is Easier Than Hate
>   *for Leymen Pérez*

A poet writes about pain, uses the scraping of veins
as metaphor, evokes Vallejo:
I do not suffer this pain as Catholic, Muslim
or atheist,

yet Catholics, Muslims, atheists, Republicans,
and Democrats, those
who practice scripture and those
who dismiss its dogma

cause the suffering of others, practice hate,
include and exclude
with a point of the finger, raucous
slam of a door.

Love is so much easier than hate, or at least
indifference: *live and let live*:
muscles rest, neurons relax, blood pressure
settles in healthy rhythm.

Try it, you trumped up sycophants, followers
of the Order of the Orange Mop.
You will be
amazed.

Lauren Camp

Tort of Outrage

Alongside another chaotic gunshot and quadrant
of havoc, the media plop down
a discussion of dead fish
on the False River. This seems to be code
for a new way to believe in complete
darkness. What do we worry about
next? The sun seeps out, silent
in its distraction. We've been so obsessed
these months, everyone stark
with angst. The trains praise
their sockets, an insistence on clanging
into the future. I turn toward brick
firmly stacked after a park
lacking all trees. Fit my realities
to a drawer in an unlocked
room. Every day, more forsaken
answers. I read of the sway of crude
oil and the many jasmine revolutions, and I slip
to bathe my hope in tranquil
emollient. How often we experience
the average—maybe victor occasionally
in birch light. "Friends" take each
volatility, subsist on spells cast
by other computers. We are all fidgeting
names fielding phone calls. Now the sky
is gray, grievous. I flick off devices and still
know another woman is captive
in a backyard container. She inches the chain
at her neck. The images are more
than I can manage. We are raging
to the oath of what we hold
against our teeth, the wound we find
infinitely open, our mutable shame.

Elise Stuart

Infrasound

Passing through forest and grassland,
roaring like a river,
beneath sandy arroyos,
underneath concrete streets,
runs a message.

The children, in deep distress,
are calling—
Locked away in metal cages
ripped from parents' arms,

a thin blanket on cement floors
no windows to look from—
the dusty ground, the bird song, the kiss of breeze
has also been taken from them.

The cry goes out—
help us, bring us back to our families.
You, who walk in the world,
speak for us,
set us free.

Steven Deridder

Opinion Spindle

Big muscles make it harder to hug,
and you've been weightlifting—
building the biceps necessary
for the necessary protection
at the redlined entrance to the club
you call home. It hits you over the head
again and again: the man aligned
firmly at the end, your position of
judgment, your one hand a flag
while the other disconnects stanchions.
You wave people over to let them go
inside without you, busy with the business
of reconnecting fabric to metal, a
promotion of fitness for the fair-armed
sidewalkers loitering afar   who are only
armed with dreams, and the values
your brand purported on a statue once

named Liberty. Still, go to the gym,
I say. You can-never know when
the wrong ends of your fists can
beat the dead horse back to life in spite
of all the little fingers you spider over
the keyboard   to make a post for
Twitter, in which you bitch about
your job, this country, your relationship—
whatever it is, all of it's the same— and then
get back to work. You survive, are the fittest,
stand by the street and continue to thumb through
the others, liking posts and giving out your thumbs-up
as you act like the only charity possible IRL
is being what you are. But you can live without
all of the fingerings. You must do something soon,
I say, for the company keeps you:
a lonely, electronic loom.

Alice Lee

Hitler's Germany

My class divided into three groups,
the perpetrators, the survivors
and the bystanders.

We read
the following novels:
Stones from the River,
The Remains of the Day,
and Canadian author
Ann Michael's book
about a Greek man
who hides a Jewish boy.
All set in various countries
during the Holocaust.

I had just returned from Germany
where my elder daughter
went to school in Berlin,

Her history professor took around 12
international students on a tour.
We visited Weimar, Hitler's East German headquarters,
toured Goethe's little writing house on the lake,
and went to the concentration camp of Buchenwald.

I didn't know
we would stay overnight there
in the officer's quarters.

Needless to say, I experienced
a sleepless night,
burning a candle in my room.

That day, we were shown
the records of all the people—
book after book after book
of names, ages, sexes, and dates
and the efficiency of the Nazis.

We saw the rooms of ovens
where they burned body after body,
and toured the hospital room
where the Nazis experimented on the children;
twins were popular subjects.
This camp has been used
up until recently with
Russian prisoners.

It was a cold and grey November day.
We rode the train. I was the mama.
I didn't speak any German,
and the pipe-smoking professor
didn't speak English, so
we sat on the train in
silence.

Note: Back in my class, one student said the bystanders were just as guilty as the perpetrators because they didn't do anything about it. This turned out to be my most successful class, taught at the branch campus of Skagit Valley College on Whidbey Island, Washignton, 1990s.

Patricia Roth Schwartz

Resistance (France 1940-44)

you chew your bitter bread
that one day you may
bake new bread

you do not lower your eyes

stealing is punishable
by firing squad
you steal a turnip
to feed your child

you sing at night
in the woods
with your friends
you dine on chestnuts
and bitter nettles

you steal an onion

you do not lower your eyes

treason is punishable by hanging

betrayal has a bitter taste

in the square you watch
your friends swing
bending the heaviest limbs

you have made a sweet stew
of turnip and onion
no salt but tears

your child has been
smuggled out so that she
make bake new bread

you refuse the blindfold

you do not lower your eyes

Karla Linn Merrifield

Cherita Triptych: Good Trumps Evil

In the new world order

we are readily expendable,
we old broads with walker or cane;

we post-fertility crones, we wrinkled lesbians,
we blacks, we browns, we reds, we yellows,
we whites— we destined for the landfills. But—

~~~

Primal dreads go unacknowledged,

so you abandon your humanity out of fear;
I have developed P.T.S.D. from the venom.

Violent poetry gathers force; poets are the first
to be hauled out and shot—Lorca, Mandelstam—
because our pens become nuclear weapons.

~~~

Nasty women write

tanka haiku renga cherita
all night   every night

so nasty women can unite
to tell the story of Medusa's mirror
in freeing millions   among them the poets

Michael C. Ford

Appointment in Pakistan

> *—After/ R. Merlin*
> *who knows how to be pro-adjective*

We are feeling maximum vulnerability. Being poets,
we find ourselves ensconced in a noble and dangerous

profession. It's like being in Pakistan, after dark. The
forces of harm's arms in company with this relentless

and reckless industry are always threatening language
commandos whose sacred weapons defend against

pronouns (as well as incontinent amateur nouns) and
belonging, only, to those who thrash their ammo. Like

Pakistani warriors, we are in the foxholes of our heads
wishing the art of battlefield journalists to be visible. All

mindless killing is an indigo Middle-Eastern desert night
of the ambushed brotherhood of busted patriots.

John Landry

American Odyssey

who will peep their head up
out of the American ruins

lived at sea-level and South enough
from Boston that I cdn't walk there

who will raise their voice
these new troubadours

who will carry their hurdy-gurdy
singing of weather here and there

and whose crops have traveled
the shortest and the greatest distance

how many masks have I to wear
to embody but not hide behind

to be empowered by and sing
the songs of love and blood

why should one man harm another
unless there is uninvited conflict

but to react-protect from assault
from unenemied strangers

or familiars trying to just take
what one has accumulated or learned

Kenneth P. Gurney

Protest

The enemy pours broken glass down our open mouths
to slice and sever our vocal cords.

It is reported by many sources that in Germany
sales of *Mein Kampf* rose sharply.

I recognize all the ghosts I feel and see
wear no clothes and appear as they did in their youths.

Trump blasts GOP over proposed elimination
of congressional ethics board.

Almost all of my progressive friends
have acquired emotional support dogs

for assistance through their political trauma,
but I want the therapist the support dogs rely upon.

Kathamann

Amen

First we will become refugees like
Tibetans, Afghans, Salvadorans, Syrians,
Sudanese.

Then our downtowns will
look like Aleppo. We will become dots
in a B/W by a National Geographic
photographer.

Love no longer surfaces in these
terranean epics. Our stewardship
is over.

Mari Simbaña

Cuttings

I only closed my clouded eyes
after they killed my father,
the soil swallowing his blood
cut hands grasping the ground
We could not run into the sky—
our feeble attempts at escape
revealed in dark dust lifting

Machetes sought out the young
chopped us down like dried sticks,
naked and forgotten in the field
They threw us in shallow ditches
Indents of yams we used to gather
where water stopped flowing,
where our stomachs stopped yearning

Men of fear sow fear with lifeless hands
eat dead flesh of our relinquishment
They have killed the memory of water
can never harvest their souls anew
so seek to fill their bellies on emptiness

They have long forgotten God made us
from soil and water
breathed sky into our eyes
gave us hearts with roots

Sisters and brothers gathered me
knowing I was alive inside
With tender hands held me together
my skin cut and rough
their tears filled my wounds

Cuttings face up, sprout shoots
all of the pieces of us replanted
green voices, a chorus to the sun
We will fill the fields once again—
quiet reverberations of Earth reawakening

Mari Simbaña

I eat my country, in hopes of remembering

I bite a hive burst open at day break,
movement of people swarming sidewalks,
hustling through intersections,
pushing in and out of crowded buses
spilling into a progressive mosaic

I taste schools of bright and uniformed children,
high-heeled ladies, men in long braids and ponchos,
babes secured onto their mothers' backs in tight shawls,
old women in sweaters gripping woven market bags

I chew long palm fronds from rising trees,
the tone of the fruit vendor's voice shouting from the curb,
a landscape of thousands of hillside houses falling
into the colonial churches at the center of the city

I swallow the radio announcer's punching words,
music seeping out of restaurants and discos,
guitar notes drifting from someone's patio,
the howling of stray dogs in the dark

Did I eat enough to sustain me when I am no longer here?
Will this flavor stay on my tongue and eyelids?
Can I contain this in my belly, when I am far away
and my heart hungers for this place?

Danielle Taana Smith

Sole Survivors

They will envy the dead as they walk among them
Identifying what remains of family, lovers and friends
They will wish they also had died in that instant
Rather than live another moment
After the 21st century atom bomb
These dangerous things exist on the earth
Lone survivors in search of others
And of making meaning
To record the human experience before their bodies melt away
From radiation
To explain to a younger generation that could evolve
That we were a complex civilization with vast knowledge and experience
Yet we chose war

Chad Parenteau

First Attack

The missiles fly faster
than you can post.

It's near-midnight.
You can't run screaming.

So you find a jpeg
of a man screaming

but now the missiles
have landed

and now that man
needs to be on fire.

When this is done
the bodies have fallen.

There are too many pictures
of bodies to choose from

and no frame of reference
no quote from coddled leader.

There are no actions left
that aren't reactions.

All you're left with
is hashtag #whathappened

Beverly Zeimer

Child Dreaming During the Cold War

We gathered around
our black-and-white Philco television,
and listened to Walter Cronkite
tell the evening news.

He knew what was happening
all over the world—
knew about the Iron Curtain,
the Berlin Wall—

We did our homework
wrapped our heads in scarves
and went to the cold bedrooms to sleep.
I might have remembered

peaceful nights in those days
instead of the dream
I'll recall every day for the rest of my life—
the Russians coming down

London Road in a military jeep,
turning into the drive and mulberry bush,
with a nuclear bomb—
despite all the plans I was capable

of making at ten years old—
turning our root cellar into
a fall-out shelter like my teacher at school said
we'd all have to do.

Gayle Lauradunn

United States History

I

Beneath the great hump
and coarse curling hair
bones bend and stretch,
shake the massive low-slung
head, move muscles an arrow
will claim for meat.
Herds four million strong
migrate to feeding grounds
carried over distance by bones
porous and thick.

II

Sitting Bull's Sioux bend
a thousand arrows to claim
the last thousand beasts.
The rest lost to rifles in greedy
alien hands. Bless these beasts
with arrows. Bury these bones
in sacred mounds.

III

Bone pickers bleed the Plains.
Sell for nine, twelve dollars
a ton the warm bones streaked
with muscle. Bone buyers make
combs, knife handles, and refine
sugar. The beast lives in your hair,
your pocket, your Sunday cake.

IV

That was then. This is now.
There will be no cake for there
is nothing sweet in erecting walls.
There will be no wheat without GMO.
Your pocket will be lined with lint.
No National Parks with a beauty
that was. The Sioux survive with
tattered lives. We look to them
to the majestic bison
to see ourselves
the shadows we will be.

Arthur O. DuBois

To Dust You Shall Return

The dust will not settle for awhile.
In all likelihood, more will be reduced to dust,
to ash, to ruin,
At least for some.

While the middle tries to hold on to a slightly higher quality of life
than the middle of thirty years ago,
who held on tightly to a slightly higher quality of life
than the middle of thirty years before,
who moved out of comfortable tenements to small single family homes
and then worked two jobs
and left their children alone more often
neglecting them 50 weeks a year
for 2 weeks at the beach
and struggled to keep it all within reach
and called it progress
until the real bosses, the invisible ones, realized
that the good work of the two loving but nearly absentee parents
could be done by another couple down south
or further down south
or to the east
and the invisible bosses could make real money
while the middle sagged.

The sad cycle is of who is placated just enough to feed
the beast of gluttony.
The illusion is that the piece of the pie has gotten bigger and more
delicious
as we merely are just temporarily
getting fattened
for the slaughter.

Tony Brown

Predation

Predation is
a lovely thing.
Efficient and
sweet on the tongue.

If a predator
becomes prey,
no matter as the meat
is no less sweet.

You aren't used to it,
are you -- this sense
of being stalked.
This sense of

teeth behind you
glistening.
Welcome to
how it is

for most. As it has been
for those who've long lived
ahead of you and
your teeth. You never

thought of yourself
as a predator and
thinking like prey
doesn't come any easier --

those have never been
your terms. Welcome, then,
to the new dictionary
of how you are going to have

to survive. Learn
*predator, prey, consumer,
consumption, product,
commodity.* Learn

*escape, camouflage,
resistance, flight,
fight, fight or flight.*

Learn or die. Remember

that you were part of this
and were oblivious
to how it worked
for a long time. Try to forget

how sweet it tasted.
Try to taste, instead, the fear
in the meat you used to savor.
Taste it on your own lips.

Kenneth P. Gurney

Run, Friend! Run!

I have laughed that laugh.

You know the crazy laugh one laughs
when the enemy's aerial machine guns
splatter eleven of your friends
all over the playground
but somehow leave you untouched
as you flip the bird at the vanishing plane.

I have laughed that crazy laugh.

Though it was not machine guns
from enemy warplanes
that bloodied that playground
or soldiers with pistols or rifles or knives.

I have laughed that crazy fucker laugh.

It comes from that place deep inside me,
that experience I have not told you
nor will I ever tell you,
because to think it is to relive it.
And I'd rather run through napalm rain
than go back into that memory.

I have laughed that crazy fucker annihilation laugh.

My psychiatric panel requests of me to tell that story,
but for their safety, I will never step upon
that playground's sticky-wet coffee-grounds black asphalt
because that laugh contains
Fat Man Nagasaki atomic-flash-destruction from on high
in my innate all-consuming desire
to save myself from that sort of left-for-dead devastation.

When I laugh that crazy fucker annihilation laugh

and you hear it. Run, friend! Run!

Joanne S. Bodin

Pontoon Politics

Floating on a pontoon boat
the ocean, like whisky and politics,
heaves random thoughts into my head
so that I can't focus on the turbulence.
Pontoon boats aren't my first choice
after election turmoil where history repeats itself
with a racist, egomaniacal, misogynist clown/puppet
whose cabinet selection is worth three trillion dollars,
enough to run their own country while they systematically
erode the fabric of our democracy.
Pontoon politics reminds me of those sleepless nights
where fog horns sound of impending disaster, and where
gentle rocking only happens in cradle memories
that have long disappeared.

Mary Strong Jackson

Surviving 45

along a chain of bobolinks
in the wake of buzzards
amidst a bouquet of pheasants
under a gaze of raccoons

an idle of politicians
and a mob of corporations
a murmuration of poor
in a shiver of homeless

flies a storytelling of ravens
a pity of doves
a glint of goldfish
with a parliament of owls

comes an army of wealth
masks of riot gear
a plutocracy of states
malignant growths of war

while a charm of finches
a dazzle of zebras
a tribe of goats
sleep with a bed of eels

under a storm of deniers
a terror of bigots
a love of liars
and stories of enemies

a wisdom of wombats
a gulp of cormorants
an army of caterpillars
a memory of elephants

wonders if we will survive

Ceinwen Haydon

Pandemonium's New Dawn

Prancing politicians of the Apocalypse thundered sound bites
Acolytes repeated tainted tropes searching for advancement
Neighbours eyed each other, suspiciously fearful
Differences were denied, or punished hard to deter others
Emotions saturated each encounter, friends became foes
Mothers and fathers stockpiled provisions for their own
Outsiders stared at empty shelves and trembled at locked doors
Newspapers replaced toilet paper covered in two types of shit
In the darkest night low, lone voices intoned sweet songs, ears pricked
Up, hurt humans heaved to remember an older world when
Mornings brought new hope each day and so at last, the tide turned

Vincent F. A. Golphin

Steel Blues (for Youngstown, Ohio)

Steel mill men at pay day's dawn,
tired-eyed, blacked or gray-skinned,
smoke and steam smudges still on some faces,
others too dark-skinned to tell,
gather at the main yard gate on third shift,
11 at night to 7, almost sunlight.
With gazes like the freed the remnant
push out in sloppy lines,
crowd closely under a dim bulb near a guard shack
to check the yield of two weeks' labor
one last time,
as behind the steel mesh fences,
back in the pits that glow against the night sky,
broad, black furnaces belch soot and fire
offer the sacrifice of hundreds' sweat and muscle
to heavens like incense or ghosts of their hopes
into clouds in the still blue-black sky.

Those who remember Youngstown mills
chant a relentless tune about bygone struggle
and hope on rusted buildings decades dormant
 to revive a way of life.

Finished for the week,
men rub green bills with thumb and finger;
those come from paid debts, no less precious,
as if dollar parchment were silk, while others
stuffed checks folded double into
hidden pockets in denim shirts, coats and pants.
They talk with vigor, survivors after all,
then march away from the light as brothers
in the struggle against the risk to live
with a threat in flame and hot ash they know is real.
One by one, many sigh as they glance at a five-foot sign
that tracks the days since an "accident."

Those who remember Youngstown mills
chant a relentless tune about bygone struggle
and hope on rusted factories decades dormant
to revive a way of life.

Eight hours in the mill easily becomes a *double* or a *triple*,
sixteen hours or whole days,
and those who cannot but accept the work call home,
tell the wives and kids in brusque whispers
that complaints have no room.
In Youngstown, needs rule.
Husbands and wives need work.
kids need clothes, braces or shoes.
The world must have steel.

Men who dance to steel blues do what they must;
behind the wire fences they bond in purpose and obligation.
Whites cut away from blacks in polite segregation outside.
They walk slowly into the dark folds of time and memory
with a wave or nod, bent backs and soot-smudged faces.

Those who remember the "Steel Valley" chant a relentless tune
about bygone struggles and hope the rusted mill remains,
decades dormant might revive a way of life.

Those who never saw the night furnace flames, weary workers
walk, nor realize the world no longer wants their steel,
know that needs still rule, so they learn to sing the blues.

Nicolas Eckerson

To the unchanged city structures

Of the poorest areas, what remains is what was when buildings were last nurtured, last used as businesses, as appraised as promising locations, signs stemming off window-fronts, companies painted in large letters in a block, and not re-painted since. And amongst all this, the inner-city, whose streets are not spoken by those who live in the suburbs of the city, of the county.

Such streets are simple in name usually, unchanged since their creation's intentions thought possibly a business district then, and as a joke, one might mention the hood, the projects, now open drug markets, supposed to be and thus the last thought to appraise the air lingering here, such businesses of another generation left as last occupied, before hope was suspended and hope was suspended because business said *peace and hair grease, I guess you'll have to survive.*

And not even someone to tear down a row of businesses past, someone to clean the inside structures break-ins passed over on the way to the copper piping. And still old grandmothers walk those sidewalks bent over, old men drive their cars under those traffic lights. In areas bereft of life, most bleak to the mailman assigned to venture through that day, that week, the most passed-over route at the station, letters showing names long-since moved to other homes. If only their senders knew where their ads, banks offering loans, credit cards, reminders about savings at stores nearby, if only these mixed-commercial letters could detect a departed place when they go unanswered for so long.

To unchanged city structures, mentioned around elections by voters voicing missions, attempts to bring attention to restore our city projects, volunteer flower-planting crews, murals painted, hope in many forms come along every so many years, but no major life-change to what memories those buildings hold *Better days, better days,* they say to anyone whose attention wanders there. *Better days, better days,* is it normal that they've passed so long ago, yet still can be felt, the lettering of the 1950s, 1960s, the time of the manufacturing booms, little niche commodities were made there, the taxes so fitting, the neighborhoods looking their most lively then. *Better days, better days,* the inner city says, the plaza malls, businesses in bare bones, cameras, bars, gate-doors close over store fronts early, open early, weathered from waves of stray drug-fueled bothering people, people in dire-straits of that life there, stores ready for another attempted robbery, though those attempts are only neighbor-to neighbor-proving, one who is desperate to another desperate one, and not worth the locality's chance.

Better days, then, and the neighborhoods re-generate faces in car windows, bus windows looking out over empty parking lots, looking over the cities and their bare appeal of sunlight on paint-peeling walls, rusting metal, I can't go on describing the urban decay, the rural is my heartland. We see such ruins in cities ancient in their name, we may or may not live to visit, if a full life as dreamed by some older wind tells of their history, such is the standing of our cities' ruins, a history not passed by years enough to be fantastic or fascinating or the only such scenes of their kind. In fact, people travel away from this that I'm writing about. These empty factories remind us of changing businesses left behind families and the sadness of the left-behind assumed to have been torn up from whatever roots were once running here.

Oh well, I drive through them, I shrug with them. I say eh, I'm here, alive with you, at this point in both our lives, this part of the city, strange times with uncertain end and conclusion, and if attention will ever come to our existence serving the greater good under the same sky. I call this my trip abroad, this is my European vacation sight-seeing, a little bit of that spent here marveling at what my oldest neighbors knew differently in our city here where I have lived to pre-adult years now.

And as I stay here, looking on for something to conclude, something to say, dreaming dreams of what memories the dying generation of our current oldest neighbors here remember the blocks that now are empty of their business, bustle, positive use and natural habitation, what was the best seen here? And will this need to be known before the next change comes to this burnt-out woods before it falls into ash, enriching the soil that lays undergrowth next.

Summer Brenner

Laid Off on Franklin Street

my name is, thank you
my name is, thank you
my badge number is, thank you
you don't know what I feel, thank you
you laid me off, thank you
laid me off, thank you
you let the people down, thank you
you with your big job, thank you
big house big car, thank you
you chop off one hand, thank you
want me to do my job with the other, thank you
you hurting morale, thank you
you laid off my girl, thank you
she come to live with me, thank you
I can't refuse OT, thank you
I got to feed the grandbaby, thank you
we need our service back, thank you
we need it all over the place, thank you
we need service people, thank you
we public servants, thank you
stop cutting the bus, thank you
stop laying people off, thank you
stop doing this, thank you
I need to be at work, thank you
we need our jobs, thank you
my name is April, thank you
my name is Sequoia, thank you
my name is Celeste, thank you
you laying off mechanics, thank you
that's a disgrace, thank you
that's a death warrant, thank you
those buses can't stop, thank you
those buses don't work, thank you
those buses filthy, thank you
I invite you to come down, thank you
I invite you to ride my bus, thank you
I work from 9 to 7, thank you
what you hearing today, thank you
we hear everyday, thank you
we hear complaints, thank you

we hear it all the time, thank you
old people can't get out, thank you
young people can't get home, thank you
we hear it all the time, thank you
you not respecting, thank you
when I speak to you, thank you
you not respecting, thank you
your face is down, thank you
your mind made up, thank you
you looking down, thank you
I'm talking, thank you
you not listening, thank you
you ain't looking, thank you
this bus company going down, thank you
20 years ago it was something, thank you
20 years ago we be proud, thank you
you give us something to serve, thank you
we serve it, thank you
now we got nothing, thank you
this company going down, thank you
it's on the record, thank you
it's on the record, thank you
the way you do, thank you
I'm voting you out, thank you
you going down, thank you
thank you, thank you, thank you

Kitty Jospé

Wait— it's not too late

> *Peace on my little town, haze-blessed, sun-friended,*
> *Dreaming sleepy days under the world-champion sky.*
> *—William Stafford*

Wait—
      points to *listen,* points out
be patient, thrusts an index at *I'm about*
to tell you or, drums its fingers under *let me explain.*

Wait until you see...
         every child
             count
in this hopscotch, where every jump matters
as the rope turns. Tag – you're it. *Wait!*
I didn't agree to those rules.

Wait, when it's not about you
as the sun rises, sets,
no matter the weather.

Weight when you're the mother begging
for a safe neighborhood, pleading
we are all fastened by gravity...

don't *weigh it,* or travel the speed of prayer, hoping
this time, something will change for the better—
don't smash champagne on the maiden ship,
firecracker a new season. Don't wait up,

wait on or not, wait in, for, until, after
way upon way...

Life circles on each present moment, shrugged
to the next. Look up at the world champion
sky, above the hazy town where we live.
It's not too late.

Mary Oertel-Kirschner

Secret Message

It's what they have to do for their own survival—
attach new meanings,
repeat them, repeat them,
until the words get scrambled:

The Biggest Crowd Ever!
Alternative Facts
Fake News
Witch-hunt
and so on.

Each day
another version of reality
marches forth with absoluteness.

My anger wears me down.

I drag my deepening depression like a lead wrap.

But some evenings—who knows exactly what compels it—
I stand still outside at twilight and
scan the indigo sky for one bright star
appearing before the others.
It's like a secret message,
just for me.
I'm reminded then:
there's so much beauty in the world.

I try to inhale it,
fill up with it,
store it like a shield against the next assault.

G. E. Schwartz

Knowing Others Have

I know I'll get by, but scared for fear
my fingers slip or shakiness and dread
might make me lose my grip. I play the
misanthrope in my own pantomime. All's
well, if I will cope a minute at a time.
Others--some others--before me understood
how all ways disappear when viewed too
far ahead, decided (some) to provide a
(print) topography, clues to the likely
road for us to choose is we resolve to
say the course. Doggedly pressing on,
it may go hard, or worse, tangle rough
in over-reaction and second-guessing.
Did they face what seemed options? I
try to practice steadiness. Around the
bend stray dazzles still distract me.
Knowing others have been HERE can guide
me back. In any case, I'm sure there's
enough examples till, awake, I'll know
I'm THERE. But, I wonder, is theirs
that Western sky aglow? Here shadows
narrow tonight along the way. Best to
rest now, till tomorrow, when, as others
have, I'll take it all up once again.

F. Richard Thomas

These Days

I think it's time
to go to the woods again,

away from clash and roar
of politics and war.

Perhaps I could even suffer ticks,
mosquitoes, and black flies,

sit around a campfire,
naked,

forget about obituaries
and my Roth IRA,

drink Pabst Blue Ribbon
and toke weed,

wasted
on what it's like

to be fearless, careless,
young again,

before the uniforms arrive.

Jared Smith

Early November in an Election Year

In the mountains by our cabin
this early November the grasses are dry
pressed low against the ground but
they are not dead, are holding tomorrow
in their roots and in their seeds blowing
against our shutters, over the coffee rock
where we have spent 30 years of mornings
without radio or television hallucinations;
and though the breezes bitter toward winter
the elk are migrating up our old dirt road
to the high country and the bears sleep now
plump in their dens filled with tomorrow.
Moose are stripping the bark from aspens
because while nutrients are scarce there is water
and life still hidden in those things that grew
last year, and though the rabbits and foxes are prey
to the mountain lion tagged and set loose among us
a lion will take only some in such a vast land and time.

It is two days until election day in Washington
a long way away across the tarmac highways of America,
and the way this valley is angled with its long cascade of time
you can't see Cheyenne Mountain with its aerials and bunkers
nor the National Labs hunkered down in Boulder Valley
nor the satellites circling above us, nor can we see
whatever it is they see, but damn it all, we're at peace,
and we too are waiting for the spring.

Mark W. Ó Brien

Incubus

It is late autumn and
Jacob wearies of nightly wrestling with the angel

making prayers and supplication
struggling with the divine

All through this long and endless night
he chokes on raised dust

at the foot of the Supernal Throne
journeying towards morning.

~

How much longer, Oh Lord, must he linger
keening for these small jars filled with pain?

He is tired. Tired of coming home each evening
opening his phone and waiting

looking into the mirror
of his sinfulness with patient trust

to be healed. Turning away he sees in detail
the plenitude of this world

his stout peasant stock helped to build
atop the suffering of others' labors.

Remembering now, the uncertainty of that
November day, when his heart made its course

towards the ballot box, for the earth,
so fleeting, so real, yet a lifetime of struggle

towards morning was seemingly gone the next day
unheralded. Maybe there is one God who is dividing

the world into monochromatic clouds he thinks?
Maybe these are the end times?

~

Pawing at the air Jacob once again finds himself
locked in battle pleading for blessings.

Blessings for water, blessings for the poor, blessings
for the first people's blessings, blessings, blessings...

All through this long and endless night
he chokes on raised dust

at the foot of the Supernal Throne
journeying towards morning.

How much longer, Oh Lord, must he struggle
over these small jars filled with pain?

~

Striking Jacob's hip the Angel cries out:
"Let me go for the day has broken!"

To which Jacob stubbornly intones
"Tell me your name! Tell me your name!"

The Angel, arising breaks free, slowly ascending
looking back wearily, he whispers:

"Another Four Years... Another Four Years..."
And so, Jacob, called this place where they struggled

"America."
Then, as the sun rose upon him

little jars of shame securely put away
in his haversack, he crossed the river

resolved, limping, and battle tested.

David Morse

Credo for Fierce Times

We celebrate this moment's leisure
silken loaves rising under damp dish towel;
play word games at the kitchen table.
For now we fear no disease.
We have the roof over our heads,
switches for lights, taps for fresh water.
We fear no landmines, no homeless
shelters, no cholera, no rising sea.
But I will protect you in these fierce times,
guard you with my own flesh
as the coconut husk guards its
treasure, as we struggle for what
is right; as you, my love, guard me.

Steven Deridder

Forms in the Aftermath

Alone under the sunrise,
coffee milks the air
with its steam,
and my mourning breath swirls
it into you.

Alone, at dusk,
I fire whiskey
into the red sky
blasting through my bedroom window,
in an attempt to ignite you.

At night, at 2am, alone, I cannot sleep;
it's been like this for months.
But until I can fall
with you, into the silence,
I will know you

deserve better, America.
You deserve better than all
the hatred and frustration
I can only give you, now.
We need to be quiet, and listen

to the ones on the outside
looking in, at us,
like vapor and sunlight
within the gaps   of things,
speaking the tongue of space-time

to illuminate our reality.
Across the sea, others can see
you   or I, or us,
easier than we can.
You have to learn this

or you won't survive.

(I don't think anyone will survive.)

Stewart S. Warren

Rolling Through

We're rolling with it—
the disconnect, taxes, details
of vampire culture, also aspirations

> of goodness pushing up
> through the temporary asphalt.
> Stay the wild course.

We maneuver
the corrugated dream,
the mysterious zero point;

> power as commodity, source
> elusive now and impersonal.
> We're rolling with it.

We watch one another
pushing the cart, leaning
toward some virtual treat;

> we watch the sleepy
> uneducated mind coming online.
> Vigilance, friend, is worship.

We mean to say love.
We go through the motions,
equilibration being established.

> The cosmic clock hums,
> plays it through in time.
> We're just rolling with it.

III.

John Roche, *Holly Wilson and Pamela Hirst at Bookworks*

Holly Wilson

Didn't Die Today
               for Jim Fish

I didn't die today
A disgruntled employee didn't walk into my workplace and start
    shooting all his co-workers
A bomb didn't explode in the marketplace where I went to buy food
    for my family
A drunk driver didn't come barreling down the wrong side of the road
    and plow right into me head on

I didn't die today
No, I woke up thinking about getting the coffee going
I thought about getting morning chores done,
What I'd like to eat, and what else I was going to do today

I didn't die today
The plane I was traveling in didn't fall out of the sky
A tree didn't crash down on me as I drove through a bad thunderstorm
A stray bullet didn't find its way to my heart

I didn't die today
I got up and made my coffee, fed my animals
Had eggs and beans for breakfast

I didn't die today
My addiction to heroin didn't come to an end
My gang rivals didn't finally get their revenge
My abusive spouse didn't finally release all his anger on me

I didn't die today
I went to work and did some shopping
I called a few friends

I didn't die today
My long struggle with cancer didn't come to an end
I didn't succumb to the hunger I've been suffering for months
    because of a drought
I didn't gasp my last breath as my aging body slowly gave out

I didn't die today

I marveled at the pink light of sunrise reflecting off a few clouds
    at dawn,
I took a moment to bask in the warm afternoon sun
I watched the moon rise in the evening and the stars come out

I didn't die today
No earthquake or tornado toppled my house on top of me
No tidal wave came rolling in and covered my village
No landslide carried me away in a sea of mud

I didn't die today
I came back home and my house and everything in it was safe
But now I'm sitting here contemplating the ultimate questions:
What are we really doing here in this life?
How did we get here anyways?
Can we ever know how much of our life is destiny and how much is
    free will?
What really happens to us when we die?

I didn't die today
I didn't suddenly collapse holding my chest as a massive heart attack
    came on
The aneurism hidden in my brain didn't suddenly burst
I didn't suddenly slip off the ladder and break my neck
    on the concrete below

I didn't die today.
But my friend Jim Fish did suddenly die today
And because of that
A part of me died today too

Lauren Camp

No Matter the Time

On a morning following thunder,
after a moon half ravaged
half pure, the people
who had become a little afraid of the earth
heard the melody of light
mesh into wind. Jackrabbits scattered
and leapt in the solitary business of eating
each line of green. The people propped up
in their bed as the day eased slowly
to light. The man rubbed out
the knots in her back, running his palms
over the chain of her spine.
He listed each practical
knick-knack of week. His hands swept
her sternum; she touched his knees.
When they remembered the mountains
being devoured by flame,
they clumped exhalations together.
The geometry of land was re-forming.
The people reluctantly offered
their night pulp and shadow
to the flaw of smoke and disaster.
They hooked deeper into each other
— one in front, one neatly behind.
Here, they reworked slow pauses,
and yawned. Sun snuck
between corners of windows.
By the barn, eight chickens nestled
and fluffed in the iris bed clucking.
After some time, the people lifted
up and out in bare feet
to the raw end of morning. No more
fathomless hours. There would be disorders
and bristles of worry. No more just sitting
with sleep in this indistinct golden house
in this rosy brooding, this peace.

Nicolas Eckerson

Survival of the Self

There are no stars tonight in my mind
though you're seeing me in the nightly moment
in my driveway, my way inside stopped,
to look at the season on the street.

The hands of our trees, waving to the sky
flagging, thanking, hands of graduating classes,
hats tossed in this air, with the ground
on their horizons, the speech just ended, so wind welcomed.

Train station, dropped off at the door and hugged,
as an optimistic young man, eternal soul defined,
come just as colors change from autumn to autumn,
making it leaf pile leaping to soft leaf pile next.

Photo-ready, I wanted to knock on doors,
this not yet so written to pass out, this night silent,
neighbors, had they seen the night? Tonight was
holiday, memorial, important to be together in it.

Definite things you're getting from this moment,
me in the autumn, I'd made it here as in our ship landing,
we all traveling together, this my stop, notice me waving,
graduated on, goodbye, thank you, steady onto my next year.

Gayle Lauradunn

Ease

In this time of death
I play Sudoku in Japanese
the round numbers of death
calm and provide ease

In the rocking chair I take my ease
broad strokes of death
paint the page
our country blemished for the next stage

No options exist for age
no options for truth
for beauty, for youth:
a world without ruth

In this time of death
I take my ease
Numbers upon this page
breathe gossamers of truth

Catherine Iselin

A Lifetime of Toiling

From a distance
I thought she was a boy
wearing skinny pants
hidden beneath an orange
floating shirt, until I noticed
a hump, looming
large on her back.

When she turned
her head around,
I saw a wrinkled face,
a face from another country-
a place once torn by war.
Bent in half her body spoke
of a lifetime of toiling
in the rice fields.

No bigger than a thin
curved stick
she kept on
walking
through
the vacant hall
of an American mall.

Georgia Santa Maria

Hospital

On the ER floor at UNMH
in tile, is a Native bear.
His heart-line signifies his life:
the road from nose and mouth
to blood and breath,
this mythological bear is alive.

My husband dozes in a bed,
his own heart-line of plastic tubes
monitor the mathematics of his signs
of life on a screen above:
this is prognosis by equation,
off key beeps and blinking lights.

Beaten, bruised and broken
by himself, fighting gravity,
the science of walls and floors
and how much vodka would it take
to knock an elephant to his knees:
the consummate tranquilizer dart.

This is as much a habit as its cause:
we've been here so many times
as to feel friendly toward the staff,
know where the coffee and the
snacks are kept, in case
I need to spend the night.

A slight cough, he is narcotized
for sleep, for detox, for his life,
curled on his side, fetal man
returning to his origins.
Upstairs, women giving birth, laboring
new babies into plastic bins,
while everybody cries except him.

Kevin Higgins

In the White Man's Clinic

A grand piano plays itself
on a giant Chinese rug
in a foyer so vast I once went there
by mistake, hoping
to catch a long haul flight
to Melbourne via Abu Dhabi.

Instead found myself in a glass palace
where surgeons do things
no one thought possible
and which, in the end, weren't;

in the process making sad intestines sing
like water-damaged concert violins,
lungs hoot like ruined tubas
in a building designed to mature
into a hotel, when it fails as a hospital
for those who can afford to die
during office hours.

Freya Manfred

Many Things Frighten Me

Many things frighten me as I age,
especially people with serious illnesses,
but I can't tell them I worry,
for fear they'll feel insulted.
They're more than their pain or crutches,
but I'm not reassured.
I'm still a girl waiting for my wheezing father
to rise from his sickbed,
where he fights another flu or cold
that could kill him.
I always feared the end of dad
would be the end of me.
Mom had tuberculosis, too,
and gasped for breath
when she tried to run or play with me.
They tried to keep their fears a secret
because Dad said I was too sensitive
and Mom said it was my siblings
who couldn't bear the misery of this world;
but the germs they told us about
invaded the house each winter,
dropping with the freezing snow,
festering in the rutted country roads,
sucking the color from their cheeks.
They needed comfort, more than I could give.
Flailing, whispering, shouting,
they tried to stay calm, and failed,
then tried again, linked by the fear
of watching others die, of dying themselves,
of losing us, and earth, this precious place,
this priceless battleground.

Sheryl Guterl

Verge

With seven decades past,
descriptors such as "old," or "senior,"
come with unexpected benefits.

I enjoy cheaper movie tickets, and
free entrance to national parks.
401K's send checks.

Wednesday train rides to Santa Fe
are complimentary. Gentlemen
may relinquish a seat.

The television reminds me,
that at this age, I may need
pharmaceutical help

for hemorrhoids, urinary infections,
rheumatoid arthritis, memory loss,
diabetes, and cancer.

These helpful medicines come with
dreadful side effects, all of which
"could cause death." Or worse.

When will I cross that boundary
from active to limited,
from living to barely alive?

Is this decade the verge?
Should I be hosting a party
to bid farewell to energetic,

and hail hello to fatigued?
Hell, no!!
I'm having the time of my life.

I leap away from the abyss.

Stephen Ellis

I Confess

Bedbugs, lice, how
the streaks on

unwashed windows
give the room

a golden glow,
not to mention all

the flies and the few
honeybees who

have no reason to
be here, all

make one feel
at home. The threat

of death in
a closed environment

encourages time
spent mostly

in the weeds
and wildflowers

that do things
with sunlight that

I have no need
to understand.

A stranger's
voice asks if its

hands I don't know
the name of, can

use my phone, but
I can only reply

that I neither
have nor need

a phone because
I talk to myself

all the time. As
we grow old,

distances between
formerly intimate

places grow immense.
When a child,

'China' was a word
in my mouth

that referred to
whatever was on

the other side of
the street I wasn't

allowed to cross
alone. Now grown,

I know there is
in expanding space

sufficient air for me
to breathe freely

for the rest of
my life, as I feel

persistent desire
go another day intense,

but unexercised.
Blue sky goes tangerine,

darkens and it is
time to return

inside my own
familiarity with

my life, in my
room, preparing

a simple meal.
Later, at my desk

words arrive
which tell me that

every care that
comes to me, goes

to compose my
current posture

that never stays
put, but cries out

through the continuous
breathing of my

skin. Everyone has
experienced this. Fullness

in the sudden
inability to speak

is my idea of
glory. I think I

will marry myself
so I can finally

embrace another
who also knows

that the Lord
who helps us live

our paralyzed lives,
loves all things

pungent and dirty
and wild, but hates

the means by which
they are reduced to

the dignity of honor
and rhetoric and death.

Jesse Ehrenberg

Here There Be Monsters

> *In the days of sailing ships, these were the words (along with drawings of fantastical sea dragons) that were used on navigation charts to designate the unexplored areas of the world's oceans.*

The mad
wind-driven
winter seas
are behind me now.
And I find myself
becalmed
under a fading summer sun,
my ship
miraculously intact.
And I turn
and look at all the
wreckage of the past,
washed up
broken
on the shore.
And wonder why,
in order to move ahead,
we always have to leave
so much behind.

And now,
I stand here
lost in metaphor,
my ship unanchored,
drifting.
While unnoticed,
the wind returns
and conspires with the tide
to pull me away
back out to sea.
Where once again
I take the wheel,
and set sail
on this
my final voyage.

And I sail past everything
I've ever known;
past memory,
past hope,
past pain,
past certainty,
to a place where time
is no longer an enemy,
and dreams and
expectations
are set adrift.
Leaving me
in uncharted waters,
ready to sail off
over the edge of the world;
a ship lost
in a sea
of possibilities.

Marc Schillace

Leaving

I would guess that getting old
is for those of us
who can't quite face dying
outright
all at once
but need to give up the senses
one at a time
here and there

Our eyesight dimming
Our hearing fading to mute
Our memory washing away

And when the senses have quieted
to almost nothing
and we are between here
and there
sitting in a stiff body
that argues with us daily
and life becomes so difficult
at being life

Disgruntled we cast off the old shoe
Finally to embrace the darkness
and the silence between stars
as the home
we left so long ago
to be born

John Roche

Joe on the Border

Friends ask, "Are you doing poem-a-day for National Poetry Month?"
Joe answers, simply, "Which nation?"
Can't always remember which side of the border he's on
Dreams he's t'other side of the Ice Wall, cave painting,
    composing his earliest songs
Friends say, "Wake up, Joe. This is the good ol' USA"
Joe can't answer border guards' questions, never has the right i.d.
believes poems should be his universal passport
With coyote instincts, glides ghostlike across borders
following smuggler routes across Pyrenees, pilgrimage trails
    across Himalayas
Knows he's only a step or two from crossing the Big Border,
    but has no fear

Martin Willitts, Jr.

Sonnet: The Lessons I've Learned So Far; Turns Out, There's More to Learn

Oh, happy life, where are you when we need you?
The fog empties visibility with steam from a colander.
The air is ripped, a chainsaw going against the grain.
Love is the last thing anyone can think of at this time.
I could make a quilt out of this night and stars.
There goes the sun retreating into the far mountains.
I could not stand learning back then.
I thought the pain of experience would crush me.

Turns out, I am stronger than I suspected. Turns out,
age makes the trees stronger. I am more certain and assured.
Of what, I am still learning. Turns out, knowledge expands
like rings inside a tree. When yesterday is behind me,
somewhere the future is putting out its thumb,
hoping I'd let it hitch a ride inside me.

Joseph Somoza

Vegetation

That tall, listing yucca
may be looking at me—
      through the hollows in the dead fibers
that make up her scraggly face,
      beneath the green brush-cut
sprouting from her head with its
three antennae that flowered recently
      and dropped their seeds.

We've been facing each other
for many years of mornings now,
      to the tune of
dove monologues, and dialogues that
sound like monologues, and finch chatter
      whenever I remember
      to put the bird seed out,
across the patch of sand where
leaf shadows are animated
      by the breezes.

Today, Memorial Day, I'm writing this
      memorial to us before I leave.
Maybe when I return you'll have
      fallen over, smashed
on cinder blocks, and I'll have to
      chainsaw you to pieces,
drag you to the curb, and leave you
      for The Grappler.

Or, if I don't return, you'll continue
sending your cockeyed looks
      toward the lawn chair by the bench
where I would sit, under mulberry boughs that,
from your perspective, might've
made my head seem to
sprout leaves. It's true
  that I've begun vegetating.

The longer I've sat here
        the more I've grown resistant
                to moving,
the weaker the allure
        of distant cities.
If I could, I'd probably take root
      in this back yard
and let the seasons
        send their annual
                transformations over me.

Roslye Ultan

The Bells Began to Ring

Consumed in the thick night of oblivion
How do I know this place, or even

Why I was born to be here… fearful
afraid to reason, afraid to be happy

Because I have encountered the white tiger
in this harsh thrum of an unvarnished world

The color of my life churned into weeping
ultramarine thumbing on the shoreline

At night an endless dream of white caped waves
heave in a tryst with the angel Gabriel

Coiled asleep witnessing uncontrollable
micro-creatures tunneling in my body secretly, silently

like the prowess of a tiger
licking blood from a spider monkey

Suddenly – life shattered into pixels
leaving little time to wait at the red light, only

drive the dim road
through liquid grey fog

A race between disappointments
and the blur of hope - of *Ohr Chadash*

Crossing the boundary of acceptance
Another chance to circle the roundabout…
toward the source of infinite energy

John Landry

Lesson in Detachment

and a third piece
of a second tooth
clinks into a bowl
after scraping my
tongue on its way

such brittle metal
falls from my head
leaving unlit niches
where food abides
and tales go untold

the dignity of aging
eludes the undoctored
and gravity unyields
the floor and the mic
for frivolous banter

Dwain Wilder

Tap Tap

My hand is too infirm now at long last
to trust to pencil or pen, though it does
well enough with the sharpest knife,
the most delicate carving, fine tweezers,

as if my hand knew that writing is too constrained,
can only be done in one posture, a habit
too old in me to even warrant
much less deserve
rehabilitation.

And so, however I flourish about in the world,
making art and life in whatever way,
when I come to preserve a thought
for later use or put it in a vessel for tea
to brew and share

I am likely to find myself sitting before this machine
these lozenge soldiers in ranks and columns,
deserting the passionate pleasures
of the hand's intelligence.

I will take up again my pencil and paper
and find in my hand, for all its failings, its muse.

Dick Bakken

Planning for What You Don't Want to Happen

First and foremost
don't panic, don't scribble a list,
and never fall asleep in a backyard hammock or
under someone else's bed. I'm warning
you because after all my 76 years of downhill skiing and upside
pinion pounding never dropping but a dime, waking like
moths coughed in a casket
not quite my own, I have finally learned
to just wait.

Martin Willitts, Jr.

Sonnet: Rain Followed Me Home

In Vietnam, it rained sidewinding.
I carried medical supplies in,
wounded men out. It rained whether
they had a missing leg, or
if the men wrote home frequently.
I swear, it rained during operations.
It rained even where cranes built nests.
It also rained if no one attacked.

I learned how to drag a wounded man
through mud into recovery. It rained
while I reached into open chest wounds.
It rained right inside more rain.
When I came home, rain followed me.
Rain kept asking for healing.

Bill Nevins

wings

feathers found scattered
on this homely maze below
some might say he flew too high

some say-- hey, soldiers die,

you know.

nah, i say,
he rises still

fire in the moon

love in his heart

laughter in his eye

Manuel González

Grief, Guilt, Gratitude

The loss of loved ones
Muerte makes mortality meaningful Reminded of our own inevitability
But grief can be
A selfish emotion
Mourning missed opportunities Moments that can never be mended
That time has ended
And
I hate myself for so many reasons
For feeling
For what i didn't do
What i could have done
Ashamed
Myself to blame
That's why i hide
Push it deep inside
Pretend it's not there
Act like i don't care
Go on with my day
Avoiding anything that would remind me Hoping my emotions never find me
I know it's not healthy But that's how i cope Avoidance
But i'm learning
To listen to the spirits around me Whispering in the wind
On wings of a butterfly
Fluttering by
A shooting star
Those who i've lost are here surrounding me Protecting
Forgiving
Reminding me
That i should be
Living

Larry Schulte

Friends for Life

Five young gay men
working on their doctorates
found each other,
super-glued the bond
that summer of heat and laughter
in Chris' apartment.
The one with air conditioning
utilities included.

John was first to die.
1982.
No one knew then what it was.
His countertenor graced
the New York City Opera, the Met.
His voice now
only a recording.
His Vicky Edie lounge act
rolled you off the couch.
His New Orleans background
brought us beignets,
coffee with chicory.
His Doctorate in Musical Arts,
posthumous.

Chris was next.
1984.
Staccato cowboy boots
had pranced across the stage
announcing his composer rhythms.
Teacher of composition.
The Denver gay men's chorus
sang at his memorial
a song that he had written.

Best friend Peter third.
1987.
Doctor of phycology,
but also ballet master.
We hunted mushrooms every spring.

117

Left Oklahoma research
for small New Jersey college
so he could die at home.
Ambulance,
St. Vincent's hospital
in New York City
to Newark,
to the bedroom of his youth.
He died, two days later,
overlooking cherry blossoms,
smelling backyard lilacs.

That left only Rick and me,
the last of five companions.
Rick long lost in the nursing home
no longer knows my name.
More lost now
than in our smoke-filled nights.

1989.
The year of my big break,
solo Soho exhibition.
The year they told me
I would die, six months to a year.
Get finances in order,
write a will.
Life changes when you expect to die.
That year the gallery director died.
I lived.

Mark Fleisher

On the Edge

on the brink of the precipice we stand,
brittle rocks the color of ash
crumbling under the weight
of ill spoken words

peering into the blackness
of the abyss, knowing
once we fall, if we fall,
rescue impossible
from the unending cavity

we had conquered the steep
face of the cliff, exulting
in the accomplishment,
planting our flag in the earth,
sharing glory with the
righteous and true
an unexpected stumble,
fingers tenuously grasping
rough-edged outcroppings

who could save us,
only ourselves if minds
remain free of debris,
focusing on redemption,
rejecting the alternative
already threatening survival

Scott Wiggerman

Twilight Time
                    —a golden shovel including a Dickinson last line (#1738)

A good day for tears, for shadows that
skim adobe walls and leave us devastated,
for skies that offer thin condolences, for childhood's
amputated crayons, and the entire trying realm

of adolescence. We are stronger now, or so
we tell ourselves, but nothing's easy
as platitudes. How many years to go, to
outlive the damages we cannot repair?

Michele Brown

Survival

how much DO we see
lying here
sun-warmed cement gardens
how much do I have to give up
to get that life I want
without all those tubes and bells and whistles
freezing my toosh off
fluoresced-dim room
cohabiting with another human life
dedicated to wheel of fortune for the rest of their whatevers

gone free doing free
gluten-free gone dairy-free done sugar-free with grain-free smattering of
fluoride-free water
How much healthy nourishment is touted as unhealthy, and vice versa
simply because people believe so easily that fast bit light news
so little fact checking because, well, LAUNdry and binge-watching
travel league baseball!
divide living into surrealviving

trying here to rid body
of pain of wakefulness of sleepiness of cancer of dying
living written into the margins in hasty black ball point pen scrawled
palms over temples fingers meeting over crown
how to work
withdrawing into aching fingers toes arms legs hips
working withal knowing data keys to freedom
a canticle to liebovitz surrendervival

giving so much life into giving up so much life to give interacting up
taking so much away from being no one recognizing any part of you
any more of you taking gentle steps within that garden walk
irradiating steps among dying weeds nee herbs
fried by the force dedicated to saving life
taking life with everything it has
breath dogged by that frustrated ache of missing/
life stolen by bully pulling strings instead of punches

how much DO I have to give up
to get that life I want to have without
all those tubes and bells and whistles
freezing my toosh off in a fluoresced-dim room shared with another human life
dedicated to wheel of fortune for the rest of their whatevers
trapped with myself knowing it was all survivavoidable.

Lawrence Welsh

The Man from AA

in practice a stroll
or side step to give
or remain silent.
some say too much
or too severe
or draconian measures
but no matter:
he arrives with a hand
with a way to escape the hell
to damper some suffering
with a path so few
will heed or believe
but a rising in the end
a rising now
for the words become fire
like old whiskey
on a newcomer's tongue

Declan Quinn

Cheer up!

Cheer up, he said.
Give yourself a shake, she said.

Take the pills, he said.
Talk to someone, she said.

Stop asking for attention, they said.
Stop putting your drama on Social media, they said.

Stop trying to tell people, they said.
Nobody cares, they said.

Everyone's depressed, they said.
Everyone's suffering, they said.

Hide your illness, I heard.
Hide your shame, I heard.

Merimee Moffitt

we do what we can

without a body to bury
without a goodbye
without ashes in the updraft
without roses from the bridge
without a funeral or burial
without an after-school snack
without bacon and eggs waiting: dad! dad!
without a father over easy
without his tools and smoke
without his smile and laugh
without his eyes or worker's hands
without much hope allowed
without his green gold eyes
without the common sense and old tattoos
without the soft link that breaks the chain
without a key or lock or door
without his love and muscular body
without a phone call or number to call
without his broken promise and his non-ghost
without finality
without tears and talking in the truck
without hugs or lunch
without touch or scent or soccer times
without this rotten drug
without rot and lies
without this fear, this hunch
without the worry that all is good or not good
without heartache leaking from feet
without his knees, and soul, and face

we do what we can

Joanne S. Bodin

In a Colorless World

In the morning the sun shines through obscurity that swirls around
and through tiny cracks barely open in a colorless world.

In the morning our hot coffee offers more than taste and aroma.
Steam rises from hot mug with no place to go in a colorless world.

But cracks can open when we let go of clamor and allow nothingness
    to be our guide.
The sun finds cracks even when color gets sucked out of humanity.

It rises every day to the laughter of a child. Knows the smell of seaweed
    and salt water.
Sees reds and oranges in fall leaves and warms tiny buds in spring.

It shines forgiveness while the natural order finds balance.
It mourns for those who cannot find that ray of light,
    even in absence of color.

Mark Granier

Sing, Words

That you may survive
those star-grazed years after I've
gone back to where I'm going: air

of a song, dead air, my dark star
set in the glimmerless hush,
cool enough to touch.

Sing, that something remain
of these epic, mundane
conversations hoofing it down my back

clicketty clack —
that you may hit or miss
with a flourish, a backdraught, a hiss

like intaken breath. Life itches to get out
of its mildewed coats,
glint with the motes turning

in a slanted beam — O sing
the slow schoolboy's daydream
counting them in.

Ezra Lipschitz

What Remains

Today… I will celebrate
the snowmelt, laughing
here in the Navajo River

Today… I will sing along
with even the irritating cries
and caws of black crows
and the Mountain Jays

Today… I will drive
the backroads below
these snow-capped
Sangre de Cristos
that'll carry me down
to my daughter's eyes,
those shining quasars
in the darks of my skies

Today… I may even rhyme
a few of this poem's lines,
but then pull out before
it's literarily too late

Today… I will drink
the water while it's clean
enough not to kill me, and
the sacred scotch—as long
as Juan continues to pour it
at my end of Maria's little bar

Tonight… I will sit by
this popping piñon fire
and remember to mostly
listen to my girl's stories,
instead of offering all my
damn good advice to her

Tonight… I will praise
the Full Worm Moon
as it hovers up over
the same piñon fire

Tonight… I'll thank
a god I wish was there
for the high desert chill
and needle-whiff of pine

Tonight… I'll play a song,
a deep, river-bottom hymn,
to the American Southwest,
my plea to every earth-force
and power of benevolence
to help us save the glory
and wonder of this place

Declan Quinn

Closer

I spent the evening walking by a water's edge.
Taking nothing in but the smells and sounds.
Rotting driftwood laying the base over two flies fighting or mating,
In a buzzing cacophony over the soft lapping of the tide.

I see a boat far out drifting rhythmically on a lonely swell.
But unlike me, it's empty, rudderless and aimless.
Or like I was, maybe. But not today.
Today I'm free to enjoy this peaceful escape, just minutes from my back door.

I used to be careful not to slip or trip into the murky black,
I wouldn't have had the strength to get back out then.
It's all me now, no pests, nobody's time but my own.
I like it here, I can just be.

Kate Bremer

Five Points of Connection

Tantra tangerine sunset
Translucent heart,
30-dollar Himalayan salt lamp,
A candled egg or batwing.

The animals cast a circle
Around us, grounding with
Muddy pelts. Shake it off.
Touch a donkey to break a spell.

Kestrel eats poem
(on the virtues of getting lost).
He ain't no GPS.

Cushion of air between us
Then, an arrowhead, Later
A cranium—armadillo!
Core of Oak, Mountain
Sacrum. Lalo is still.

There are those who
Would destroy animals and creeks
And hate the poor.
That is a fact.

Vulture in Latin
Means purifying wind.
White winged doves and cedar
Branches riffle my hair.
Cathartic breeze.

Blanco, Texas

Kate Bremer

Prayer Blanket

As if prayer were an inquisitive burro
Turning over the hay cart of beauty,
Or one stout mare—a psalm of earth,
A balm, a tongue, a gong for you.
My prayer is one of distraction—
Heat lamps, duct tape and PVC,
Damn wind and winter reactions,
Crinoids, stone mollusks and pollen seed.
What yucca spears stand to offer,
Basket strings and drawing tools.
"Kestrel", my burro's radiant fur,
Pictures in the sand. We are all God's mules.
Fools? What part of the desert will sustain?
Lichen, limestone, and the donkey train.

G. E. Schwartz

Balm

Mid-morning film over the dayshine
has incidentally opened the ear to little
clanks and whirrs out there, the hum
of world going on, untroubled by that
silent witness, sky. We here are silent.
Yet being drawn into, with, each creature,
each machine-work thump, each step, faraway
bark, buzz, whine, rustle, etc. gives our
place a voice, dampered by distance; serves,
through outer windless openness of skywash,
to open a bud of tremulous hearing. Full
day will blare away later. We know we will
survive it, and to do it, then, we'll walk
(at an even pace) where cars, trucks making
deliveries, past a construction site, kids
out of school, and a dog lapping at a water bowl
outside a cafe, walk through that mix, a mix
most studios would take pride in. Then we'll
go steady for our own sake and the others on
the sidewalk burrowing by. And we'll keep our
face like anyone's, in pedestrious preoccupation--
although we'll have to part our lips a little
to play in. First, we'll test the pitch of the
prevailing din (humming) then (still with no
perceptible opening of mouth) intone on the same
tone-level with all the enveloping street-sound.
LOUDER. As loudly as we can! Nobody hears a thing,
even ourselves! Otherwise surely someone would
give that glance of furtive avoidance that flicks
some flushed and angrily gesturing man you may
hear shouting along anywhere about town. He chooses
to stray apart from this condemnable crazy world.
Before you know it, surprisingly, evening, after
the harsh hours of sharp light, will close in
with overcast. and the thunderous busynesses
WILL shift to calmer surge and flow. Before dark
(sky and windows contemplating emptiness) we'll
half-hear a freight-train passing over High Falls
and remember the near great lake, and the coming
balm of the night.

Mary McGinnis

Yes, Little Mind

You are not dying, only in-
evitably changing-
surrender to the slow progression;

lift into 40 days of quiet;
in the beginning it was a birthright; now,
touch each day for a moment of quiet
tell yourself that it came to you
like a mysterious
evening bird.

Make room for that bird; know
it intends you
no harm; let
darkness pave the way.

Margaret Randall

Younger Than That Now

> *I was so much older then. I'm younger than that now*
> —Bob Dylan "My Back Pages" (1964)

Great hands holding seasonal scales
rise and fall
as they are touched by babies' births
old clocks and spring rains.

A gaggle of tiny Peregrine mouths open
to mother's repurposed offering,
crowd the nest
perched high above our hope.

Hope fades when we forget such scenes,
revives when memory paints them
in vivid color, malleable tense.
No politician's rant can take their place.

Younger than that now, I am ready to use
this image saved from ruin.
Older then, I almost missed
its promise.

Maril Nowak

Switching Off the News to Observe Crocus

There have been times, easily chalked off to innocence,
when what was said was meant, others when the rude rush
learned a thing or two, subdued and fit for company—
the child who fights twin imps, Play and Itch, and quietly
sits at table through all five courses; or the sermon yawning
into overtime without a winner, nothing but an inkling that
the earth might prefer to breathe through funky water, soul-
singing its gibbosity in great gasps, the way a frog re-blinks
the start of us caught listening and rising to the beat, or
the way a poet may become a foul-weather church attendee,
such as Wendell Berry. Once again, the crocus have punched
through frozen mud to assault our starving eyes with color.

Wendy Heath

Deer

The stars are falling
from your country's flag
into the lap of your little girl.

In crow light
Grandmother
suspends each star
in the air round the child.

Deer's tentative presence.
Breath, salt.

Mary Dudley

The Mountains Watch

The wind rumbles over the roof,
and outside the window
a whirlwind of dead leaves swirls,
its grit pelting the glass.

At the foot of the escarpment
the river threads its brown way south,
leafless *bosque* bordering the water's ribbon.
Everything is brown.

Skip the rooftops of all those structures
on the valley floor.
Look across those treetops
to the foothills—bare and rounded mounds,
hunkered below the snowy mountains.

The world's in turmoil;
uncertainty's the only thing
that's certain.
Guessing at what's coming, and fearful of the guess,
take comfort in the wind's strength,
the way the trees bend beneath its power but don't break,
the way the mountains wear their heavy mantle, silent, watching.
Take comfort in their ancient calm.

Janet Eigner

Motherhood in the Mountain Mahogany

The deep-green Mountain Mahogany that husbands
tiny leaves year-round, rests against a windowed wall.
Branches groan in screaming wind, chafed against stucco.

A Canyon Towhee nests low in its branches,
showing only pushed-up tail and russet head
past the tight semi-hemisphere of eggs and twigs.

Early spring snow swirls wet, thick and sideways,
keeps us nesting too, warm by the woodstove.
Five decades wed, pledged to four-season weather.

The male sails out from his leafy guardpost,
beeps a warning against our presence.
Joe peeks behind the pleated window shade,

says the Towhee has a layer of snow on her back.
We live the best and worst of life's storms as well.
Couldn't catch the one that fell from *our* nest.

Linda Yen

The Second That Flew By

The hawk perched on the edge
                of the patio cover
is spewing feathers
                      of the mourning dove
across the wooden slats
                a drift of down
thicker than snow
                lighter than blood
clotting the air
                this far inside the city
where we thrive
                on daily doses
of snapchats & trumped-up news.

I could sweep away
                the feathers mounting
like the latest body counts
                remember driving
I-40 towards Gallup
                how cloud shadows draped
across the mesa
                morphed from horse
to cougar to crocodile
                melted in the bleaching light
the valley so parched
                you could taste the dirt
coat your breath with it
                carry it home
like a mound of feathers.

It's nature's way
                of mopping up
my knuckles glared
                as my broom scraped
against cement.
                By the cinder block wall

I scrambled the odds
           dumb as my neighbor's
newly trimmed hedge
           to the second that flew by:
a shudder of wings
           its mate's startled cry
eyes angled at me
           as if I owed it
an explanation
           as if I, too,
had shared in the spoils.

Gretchen Schulz

Tornado People

As he lets her come home time and time again
one man after another, his stomach churns like a
riptide swirling pulling him under, he feels defenseless
acceptance is a shore in another hemisphere
riding inside the dark beast all perspective is lost
he is unreachable, generational lies and addiction flow
like old blood through his veins, besides there is a child to
raise and not enough money, he's looking into a gaping hole
a lioness waits to swallow a smaller him, tornados rage across
the plains coming going changing course coming again, he dodges
ducks looks for safety, confusion is en-route to paralysis, unsafe
territory looks like home, fingers cling to the edge, all children
are terrified of abandonment, reliving a dead parent's
undoings he builds walls praying
the prayer of distraction
begging for better
If only he
knew by
accepting
the tragedy
he'd be
set free
letting
go of
the monster
on his back

Mina Hatami

The I

Soft, warm, body
Gorgeous and tender
Full of lines and curves
Chalus Highway*,
In between the mountain and the canyon

My body,
Loaded with danger
Rough
Hidden underneath the armor

My frame, scared, without protection
Full of horror
In need of a safe place

My body
The invisible wild flower,
       that grew in graveyard of suffocation.

Graveyard, place of death, silence
    opposing greenery
        growth
            life

Choose!
Death? Or life?

      life in death
      life in graveyard
No!!
Death in graveyard!
This is the place of death and silence

Where do you come from?

From baba's home,
    baba who suffocated
From mom's home,
    Momon who did not see

From home of a culture,
        That was in love with masculinity
From the streets,
        in which the guys' hands, passing by
                could violate the girls' bodies
                and the violated me
                      with my loan option of yelling:
        asshole!!!!

In this cemetery, I do not die
In this cemetery, I grow leaves

In this graveyard, I am not silent
        From top of my lung, I yell
        not from frustration
            but strength
                excitement
                    being alive
                        being in love

My body, daring,
    thirsty
        laying hold of all that's good

My body, in command
        bereft of all covers,
            bare
                dominating

Your graveyard, did not kill me
Your graveyard, for years, kept me under

And today
    Aged like a choice wine
        I am done!
Have a sip!
    drop by drop
        Taste life, in my smooth red

* *Chalus Road is an interstate around and through the mountains. It connects Tehran to the northern region near the Caspian Sea.*

H. M. Aragon

The Dark and Light Side of the Moon

Women gather children,
small worn shoes, a mason jar of coins.
They search in the dark night for shelter.
Española   Santa Fe   Tesuque   no roof no safety.
    I walk through galleries
       on Canyon Road, San Francisco Street, Artist Row
       to see art in paint, sculpture, and wood.
Women gather children,
cloth for diapers, bars of soap, a cooking pot.
They search in the dark night for foreign borders.
Syria,   Guatemala,   Afghanistan   no roof no safety.

Veiled women   Aphrodites in burqas   together, always together.
At the market they buy chickpeas for hummus,
aubergine for baba ghanouj, fresh greens, and beets.
'Morality Police' flog their bruised legs with long-handled batons
if the women move too slowly, if they cause men to lust,
if they…if they…if they…
Women are beaten because they are women.

An art collector at the Santa Fe farmer's market
wears Versace sunglasses. Make-up hides her blackened eyes.
    I fill a straw basket with fresh squash-blossoms,
      hard crust bread, goat cheese, fresh sweet corn.

My first-grade teacher, Miss De Boise,
sends me home for an absence note.
I walk through the park   alone,
through the small town,
into the countryside.
A man follows at a distance.
I hide in deep damp furrows
between rows of corn stalks.
He darts back and forth   searching.
I crawl home on my belly,
mud-stained dress,   my heart a bass drum.
The scent of corn forever scorched on my brain.
Today, in my dreams a field of sweet corn is a safe haven.

Jihadists abduct Nigerian girls from a boarding school.
Western ideas   western studies   forbidden.
Oh sweet Jude Thaddeus, apostle of lost causes –
there with Jesus in the boat   on the hill   at the supper –
Bring Back Our Girls!   from the Boko Haram.

In schools from six to sixty. I study art, music, poetry.
My soul transforms, closer to God – a whirling dervish.
Sounds of reed flutes, drums, cymbals.
Whirl   whirl   white skirt flies   tall honey-comb hat –
farewell to mind.
Rumi,...*what is this whirling...caught in the wind?*

In this container I call body   there is peace.
Arms open wide   I see God in every direction.
Whirl, right arm up   closer to God,
left arm down – I pour women's sorrow into the ground,
ground where at the far end of an open field
three ravens prance back and forth on a rail fence.

Colleen Powderly

By Dark Light

In my shadow life I have healed women of pain by simply touching
    their hands, cupping a cheek with my palm.
Resewn buttons on their shirts, with a thin

braid of my hair, leaving durable repairs with my particular mark
on their garments, their lives. In that life I have been unafraid of
    loneliness,

recognized it as the natural state for women grown too strong
for the world. Its rib tug is less acute because I wear easily

the energy that flows out from me unshielded in the light of day,
increases its potency each afternoon,
    slides carefully into bed each evening.

Thirteen times each shadowy night I rise, face the moon with
    raised hands,
pull her power down my bone and ligament frame, broadcast it

back to the ground to join with the sun's, enter walkers' feet,
    give their strides strength.
I keep some with me, morphing the coal of my anger

to a jeweled source of light so some nights I beacon safety
for streetwalkers earning their children's morning meal.

I move into their shadow lives and we save each other.

Elaine G. Schwartz

The Flautist
       —After *"El Flautista," Remedios Varo, 1955*

Eyes closed

mask studded with ocean pearls

the flautist leans against gray granite

her music   soft as sighs

raucous   as humanity's lies   worries

the world's unsettled breath

as shards rain upon the earth

scatter at her feet   fragments filled

with skeletal fish splinter   trilobites tumble

upon thirsty soil   faceless shards

mark sedimentary time

and the flautist plays

and hubris flows into the dark

oily miasma of our own making

Jane Lipman

Unsung

It is late at night. You are by yourself,
a nurse heading home from the late shift.

You step out of the subway, inhale the acrid air,
push the turnstile. Glancing up the steps,

you see the gleam of a knife. You climb
the stone stairs, address the man hidden there:

Excuse me. It's late and I'm scared.
Would you mind walking me home?

After that, he waits at your subway stop
every midnight and walks you to your door.

Jennifer Maloney

Detained

There are no door handles
in the back
of a patrol car.
I didn't know.

I wasn't cuffed, so
when you started to say
when you started to tell me
do it
take off your top
show me
show me your tits I reached
for it I reached
for the door handle I reached
and you

smiled.

Inside my belly something curdled.
Broke off. It was shaking
and sharp. It
slithered
sliced
serrated its way
up the back of my throat,
up and out. You

had driven to the gulley
the ravine where mama said
she told me

don't go there
don't go down there
that's where the hobos live they'll
hurt you
down between and if one drifted
up from the bottom she called

she called the cops
like you
like you to help us keep us
safe

from harm and you said
show me
show me your titties
I'll let you go
just show me
show me your pussy I'll
let you leave but touch it yeah
touch it suck it and you'll be
free
you won't get hurt yeah
you'll be
safe
if you do it
do what I say

You
watched me
in the rearview mirror eyes
disembodied just a pair
of eyes that watched and widened like
maybe god's eyes
watching
judging
taking possession owning
my body.

I turned off then.

No door handles in the back
of a patrol car no way out no way
to make it stop so
surrender
surrender
lay back and enjoy it you

took the money you
take the chances you
pay the price if you pay
the price I'll

let you out
I'll let you go you'll be
free
you'll be safe

okay.

Here they are. My titties.
My pussy here
it is you can have it here
my mouth fill it with yourself and I
will do
as I must do
to keep safe you'll
let me go you'll
let me out officer and
I'll be safe but guess what

guess what I am safe here
down in the gulley down
in the ravine I'm a hobo and I can run
run
run
I am free

no door handles here to lock me in

look at my pussy
look at my titties
here they are but I am gone and I am
free

like a hobo hopping trains and drifting
drifting

gone
safe
free

Karla Linn Merrifield

Breaking Silence

For a messy (I peed my pj's) and terrifying (à la Kafka) moment,
    I sang.

I, who cannot carry a tune in a tote bag, sang like a canary,
    albeit one in a coal mine.

I, the one offbeat, arrhythmic, warbled a mezzosoprano aria,
    the heroine's warning

of chaotic incompetence and amoral lust for robots and
    drones swirling

in the maelstrom sweeping across the land far above my cage
    in the dark pit

of imagination— for I, Serinus canaria forma domestica,
    fly beyond

the bituminous West Virginia mine of my willing captivity,
    trilling the future.

Janet Ruth

Song for Us Who are Working Our Way Through

—After D. H. Lawrence's "The Song of a Man Who Has Come Through"

I.

I have lost the path.
We all stumble, as a whirlwind engulfs us.
A roiling, towering haboob obscures
the way toward that more perfect world of which we dream.
If only we could see our hands in front of our faces.
If only we could keep the dust and tears out of our eyes.
If only we could rise, stand before it.
Most terrifying of all, we fear being lifted, kidnapped
by mindless, heartless chaos that destroys
resistance—that muscular gift.
We twist and bend like a tree before the hurricane.
With a cold Smith & Wesson M&P 9
we are pistol-whipped, shot in the back.
Will we crack?
Will we crumple?
We tumble through a pandemonium like Bosch's Last Judgement.

Anger blisters our souls,
our fury battles despair.
We are alone in a throng of losses.

What are the thundering hooves on the hill at night?
Is it someone coming to rescue us?

No, it is The Four Horsemen.
Can we survive?
Can we survive the storm?

II.

But I burn.
A firestorm sweeps through us.
A fine flame ignites a revision in our trajectory to the future.
If only we can tend the fire, ride it, if only it carries us.
If only we can be flammable.

Most powerful of all, we can offer ourselves and be consumed
by the fine blaze that burns
clean
through our present chaos.
Conflagration—a firebrand gift.
Like fine, steely plows beaten from abandoned swords,
we are strong, sharp-honed like the plow's share.
Soil will turn past the moldboard, we will sow the seeds
of a more peaceable kingdom.
Hope vies with despair.
We would be lovers, embrace diversity and justice,
blur no truths, exclude no huddled yearning masses.

What is the cry at the door at midnight?
Is it someone who wishes to do us harm?

No, it is that future we seek.
We cannot sit and wait for rescue.
We must rise up, we must open the door,
let it in.

It is the storm,
or rather—

    we are the storm.

Ray Johnson

Let Us

Let us mellow
Let us chill to the bone
Let us quietly chant
Universal bop and beat
Let us not give up
      be not to tough
Let us rest before next sunrise
Being utterly silent
Let us......

Let us bring this sunrise to sleepers
Heaping great goodness and
      unsaddled intention for day's awaking.
Let us protect our vision which is
      unique and shared with those
            turning over from dreams.
Let us always and ever go forth
With attention so constant that
None dare blink. Let us.....

Kate Marco

subversive

singing loudly
as I rode my bike,
'AMAZING GRACE,
HOW SWEET THE SOUND…..'
I found a truth
upon the faces,
of the people staring,
as I passed each one:
it is subversive
to act joyous
in public.

let's declare a day
void of speech,
when our responses must be sung,
let's pull the red noses
from our pockets
and wear them through security,
let's buy flowers
for the next person in line,
let's stand on soapbox
reciting odes to the world,
let's give all the money
in our wallet
to the next person begging,
let's empty our cupboards
to feed the hungry,
let's sing
in our gardens,
in voting lines,
riding the subway,
driving our cars,
riding our bikes,
'AMAZING GRACE,
HOW SWEET THE SOUND…..',
loudly
and
joyously
subversive.

Lauren McLean Ayer

Lullaby

A world like this could make a girl
      agoraphobic.
Especially one who at the age of four
began her very own
      memorial roll call list
which has now grown so long
      she has forgotten her own name.
"Sometimes," she says,
"I want to wall myself into
      this tiny casita,
while others,
I want to run through the streets
      naked and on fire
burning all death
      from the world.
But usually, I just sit in my room
      watching streamed TV
      to drown out the noise
and do my best each night
to rock myself
      to sleep."

Lyn Lifshin

The Geranium

I am going to stop thinking
of the I'm sure dead geranium.
I know it's come back, like
a love you want to keep on
with since it seems there's
been so much you've been thru
together. The wild red flame
flowers, even before any
buildings burned, before any
thing burned in me so wildly.
It's only a plant, not some
one dying in a colorless
hospital room, their body
enough like a flower in water
that already smells. I kept
this flower going like an affair
I put too much in to leave.
And now I'm left with
what's dead

Alexis Rhone Fancher

Tonight We Will Bloom for One Night Only

Tonight you must plow me a respite between the moonflowers,
mock orange, night phlox, and Epiphyllum Oxypetalum.
You must open me to the summer night like cereus.

You must pick my perversions like petals, allow them for one night
to bloom, frangipani wafting, a concupiscent wind
humming at my door.

I've surrendered to your heady sweat of primrose, plumeria,
addicted to your outstretched arms of night-blooming jasmine,
my heliotrope buds hard and wanting, reeking of Madagascar vanilla
with its accompanying moral ambiguity.

I am more than a day lily.

We are each bodies, hard-wired for pleasure, destined for momentary
blooming, then extinction.

When the bats swarm and the moths sidle up to this one night of
fevered pollination, let's be ready.

Let's face them, our appetency the headlights they slam into
again and again.

We will make our escape at first light. Singing.

Robbie Sugg

Some Eden

These dreams
long past
the unthinkable
    red line
        wrong
        time nor the
            place for

            buying into
       the narrow road
    is out
            of the
            question
                granted
            a spread of lupine
            to appease the shoreline pollinators
            recommends roots
                be put down in
            these and other
            pursuits considering
            the breathless yesterday's

            back-to-the-land is relative though
            bountiful the fruits of luxury
        be accounted for there are
            bills to be paid in Paradise

IV.

Courtesy of Gretchen Schulz, *Building the Cabin, 1956*

Demetria Martinez

Inauguration Day, 2017

A Mexican nun once
told me: to refry beans
add a touch of milk
if you don't have lard.
Remember that, friends,
write it down, write down
all such tips from foremothers
who lived through such times,
who knew to add extra
onion for flavor, still more
onion to stretch the meal.
We have so many to feed
and ourselves to nourish,
gathering strength to pull
the curtain behind which
the conqueror cowers.
Hot tortillas, splendid table.
We hold hands, say
the blessing: pass
the pepper, pass
the salt.

Bill Nevins

Cutting It So Close

Leonard Cohen chopped carrots
well
not a finger lost

Leonard lost his money
then sang for us to make it back
had regrets joys memories
did not forget
lived well
loved
died
but
left us his best album
ever
You Want It Darker

Good man Leonard.

So look—
we are here now
chopping carrots
slicing truths

whatever happened
happened
it ain't happening now
now is happening now
let's get it right
and get it best
chop chop chop

Deborah Coy

Half-Life of a Fruitcake

I've heard you don't truly die
until they stop saying your name.
However, I was not named
for one-hundred-six years
I persisted Twinkie-like in a rusting tin.
They use my name generically,
"a fruitcake."

Not like the ongoing story
of Lincoln, or King, or Sacajawea
who live on in your mouths.
When Robert Scott shuffled
off to history books
I stayed behind and made
him live again by surviving him.

Safe, paper-wrapped, and
hidden behind years of dust.
Like honey, molasses, and dry mix Jell-O
that can last beyond doomsday,
my candied cherries and
whisky-soaked nuts
pass the time intact.
I am returned to the historic shelf.

If placed beside plutonium
I would survive, I would become it—
share its half-life—
light up the first cockroach
that makes it through
the disintegrating tin.
Entropy does not devour me—
I am my own fountain of youth.

You will go on and on
like a far-off train whistle
through your children's voices
and in the stories your grandchildren tell
but someday you will leave those mouths
and I will have outlived you.

Patricia Roth Schwartz

Carol, Baking Bread

I delect this gift of bread,
a long flat salt-encrusted rustic loaf
from the bakery where my friend
works, her second job. She can use
the money, but really, I think
she loves it for the way the air
in that close, warm room becomes
fragrant, how butter creams its way
into flour, the pouring in of honey,
vanilla bean, cardamom, caraway.

The work of her hands a poem,
the poem a sacrament.

for CJK

Mary McGinnis

Stay, Time

Stay, this time for eating corn chips together,
telling our common pain; this
afternoon firm and reassuring as tofu;
young we are not but

the house of staying alive is strong;
I have room for my sister poets, utmost in my
memory. We had a little rain and snow this month;
we can still buy fresh
eggs and organic, cotton socks.

Loren Niemi

Thursday Morning

I've read a dozen poems this morning
And not one seemed to be worth
The posting on ubiquitous social media -
They were scattered missives for doing
Laundry and Zen sweeping a kitchen floor,
Notes for packing or unpacking the bags, or
Paying the bills. That said, reading poems
Is also living; a pause while being present.
The being present a lifeline in choppy waters,
A singular realization that we need not
Drown, that sometimes it is enough to be
Still, to feel the buoyancy of love. or
Laughter. or the breath before shouting
Out we are here and as we sight the boat.

Steve Tills

Occasionally Poems

My reputation will outlive me
whether it is good, bad, big, small,
or deserved. Somehow I
just plain know
that I cannot write about
anything specifically or deliberately, though
I must write something about something
in my way sometime or another.
Even he does not need to watch the TV
in order to understand that no man

or woman is an island,
and the Galapagos' race to a finish
line now moved daily. Even with this
in mind, how keep the little
ones and the mute
ahead of the curve
balls. There's no courage in it,

money. I mean to say, there's no care
for it, reputation, whether immortal
or self-published. I mean to say
this will not ever have closure,
crying tears or no.

Alecia Lutrario

An Ode to the Initials Carved into the Bridge

you are the permanent reminder
of something that was probably beautiful
and maybe still is

an etching of giggles and
interlocked fingers

you were probably created on a summer day
maybe august
with families and puppies and laughter
all around you
you were carved from the love of
two people who probably did not know
anyone else was there.

they may have only been in love for just a few months
the kind of puppy love that hold the naivety of lasting
I hope they did

I hope every summer they back to this bridge
maybe alone, or with their children or a picnic basket
I hope they look back at your carving
and smile

but if they don't;
if life does what it often does
if drifting is inevitable
your reminder of something bigger
will still be there

and I will do the smiling for them

William Heyen

Sustenance

I'm marooned on an island only my chainsaw for company I keep
    felling palms

it runs strong never needs oil or runs out of fuel its blade never needs
    sharpening I

 can live here my saw cuts into milk ... but I'm lonely, lonely,
    not for you

but for vellum & pens for my journal for cursive for candles for Walt
    & Emily

so I've no way even with such a saw to satisfy the longing in me until ...
    what is that water-

proof cask washing ashore? ... I might soon possess thanks to Poseidon
    what I'll need to live.

William Heyen

Achilles

Another such heaven, my afterlife in a bookshop, I meet
    & introduce

a blind poet who seems to remember & can sound the timeless siege
    & burning of Troy,

noble Hector dead & dragged in triumph & disdain outside
    that city's gates

in a dissonance of death made bearable only
    by song.

Fred Whitehead

Salvage
>   for Christy Tapp

Every Midwestern town seems to have one:
a junkyard just outside the city limits
vast bonepile of rusted frames and engine blocks
before you take a cutting torch to them
you have to make sure the gas tank is disconnected
so the entrails of the machine don't explode
during the 10,000 autopsies performed there

This is true also of our people's heritage:
the state historical society libraries
usually inhabited only by the genealogy ladies

In spare afternoons stolen from work, brittle pages of
Victorian acid-paper pamphlets crumble in my hands

One might as well be scratching in the sands of Egypt
for any small bits of memory saved up on papyrus

Once I went to the Maple Grove Cemetery in Wichita
to visit the grave of Sockless Jerry Simpson
Populist Congressman from the State of Kansas

Someone asked him: "Did farmers really burn corn for fuel in 1890?"
"Yes, and by that light they read the history of the Republican Party!"

I inquired of the man at the cemetery office
how many people ever came to visit Jerry's resting place:
"I've been here thirty years; you're about the third or so."

Perhaps we are only eccentrics in our love for all this
but at least we have "kept the faith so pure of old"
carrying a vision of the Day of the People with us always
in the cortex of our brains, in the muscle of our hearts
and in the scarlet marrow of our living bones

David Landrey

Consciousness Suite: XXXI

> *Only the camera angles change, and the solo voices of uncomfortable thought sink into the chorus of a collective and corporate consciousness, which as McLuhan well knew, doesn't "postulate consciousness of anything in particular."* —Lewis Lapham

> *To write at all is to dwell in the illusion of language, the rapture of communication that comes as we surrender our troubled individual isolated experiences to the communal consciousness.* —Robert Duncan

No communion in this
corporate set
    of mind
no vision
only sights set
to dominate the collective
    body
bomb sights   smart
    oh! hurt
in name only
of the unholy choir
wherein no true voice
stirs thought no
particular sense of
    life

but we WILL
surrender
      to love
        ever
building community
    spirit
breathing sense into
one another into
the corpus of our days.

Orin Domenico

Amid the Daily Dirt

Ginsberg is dying
Terminal liver cancer
I get the news from TV
At three in the morning
How strange,
My middle of the night vigil
Broken by real news
Amid the daily dirt
Something that touches me.
Allen is one of my fathers
For a moment I want to cry.
Long ago he put his queer shoulder to the wheel
Always a freedom fighter
Lover of words and truth
Dark beauty of cities and sex
Dark horror of America.
Child of the old Jewish Left
White beat father of the 60's and me.
Howl of anger
Bearded beatific smile
In '66 before my first peace march
With finger cymbals taught me
Hare Krishna, Hare Krishna.
Was everywhere on the streets of New York
Black beard flowing hair and clothes
A mad monk with cherubic grin
Dope smoking acid dropping guru
Bigger then and older
Than the forty-one or two he must have been.

I wish I knew then that I
Wanted to be like you Allen
Wanted to use words as weapons
Wanted to cut through the shit
That poured through the tube
Out the smokestacks
Off the assembly lines
Onto our platters
Grease and plastic
Oil and lies

Plutonium and bullets
Blanketing the cities and fields
With shit shame and ashes.
I loved men like you and Henry Miller
Who wrote of air-conditioned nightmares
Cocks and balls
Cunts and asses
Jazz and gissum
Whores and holy men.
Maybe if I had known then
I would have let you touch me deeper
Down beneath naked fear of my body and voice.

I saw you last September in Jersey
An open tent on a sunlit Saturday
Golden leaves fading flowers white contrails and
A chorus of baaing sheep in the woods beyond,
Sat two hours for a seat in the second row
Waiting and talking with a group of glowing young people
Who loved you too,
Strangely a celebrity now
For a truth-starved generation.
You arrived feeble shrunken
A bit crabby perhaps impatient with all the fuss,
So many demands on your dwindling time.
You fairly growled at silly questions,
Led us in a meditation,
And, slender body rocking sang Blake's Tyger in a voice
Remarkably resonant and somehow older than seventy,
"Did he who made the lamb make thee?"
That is how I will remember you finally
Little old man in pink shirt dress slacks and tie,
Bardic cantor bellowing Blake
In a ancient voice
Transparent angry angel of sodomy and blessed sin.

4/4/97

Ed Sanders

On the Way to Allen Ginsberg's 92nd
Birthday Celebrationat the Howl Gallery on E. 1st
June 3, 2018

—for Jane Friedman

I stopped at the bench on the edge of
                      Washington Square Park

just across the street from the old NYU Main Building
with its row of Corinthian columns
                along its 8th floor balconies way above me

where on a spring day in 1964
I wrote a melody line for Blake's
                "Ah, Sun-flower, Weary of Time"

after I had read that Allen Ginsberg back in 1948
had experienced a vision where William Blake's
voice had sung "Ah, Sunflower,"
            and "Oh Rose, Thou Art Sick..."

One of the first
books
        for my Book Boat

had been the Modern
Library

Complete Blake
& John Donne

w/ intro by
      Robert Hillyer

and on the day
I wrote a melody
      to "Ah, Sunflower"

I sang with it
      open on my lap
            on the bench

& then it became the first Fugs song
when Tuli & I formed the band
            a few months later.

Meanwhile the 92nd Ginsberg birthday
went very well, with a defiant & emphatic
reading of "Howl" by the audience

& I sang my "Song for Allen"
Simon Pettet perfect-toned
      the exquisite nature lines of "Wales Visitation"
& Eileen Myles read Allen's poems
         like a sequence of gems
            with just a touch of her Boston accent
& David Amram was on hand
         for a well-done set
         with perfect timing
              at age 87
         with his son Caleb on congas

            —Ed Sanders

Jules Nyquist

How to Send a Petroglyph into the Future

Five hundred generations into the future
humans will try to decipher the remains of our blasts
by the signs we post outside our nuclear waste sites.

Will language be forgotten
like how we decipher petroglyph symbols
from ancient civilizations peeking
between our suburban sub-divisions?
Volcanic rock in Albuquerque shouts in silence
among hikers and preservationists.
How can we be sure what is buried there?

The Waste Isolation Pilot Plant
contains two million cubic feet
of radioactive waste buried half a mile deep
in a two-hundred-fifty-million-year-old salt deposit.

We are dumping our nuclear sludge until 2070
when we will seal the area
surround the plant with obelisks
with warning messages in Spanish, Navajo,
Chinese, Latin, Hebrew
and English.

Shouldn't we include a few petroglyphs?

Freya Manfred

On Carpinteria Beach

On Carpinteria beach where the Chumash lived for 10,000 years,
saltwater washes across shells and seaweed,
erasing tiny air holes where mussels breathe and wait,
and rivulets of black pitch once used to make canoes
ooze from ancient pits along the shore.
Ten years after Spanish ships arrived with long guns and smallpox
a few Chumash were left alive, while thousands
lay buried in the Mission, bone on bone.

Now, laughing dogs chase seagulls across the sand,
and surfers in slick wetsuits park their pick-up trucks
and trot barefoot into the rising waves,
while scientists from the university peer into tide pools,
jotting notes and muttering,
and white-haired men and women in tennis shoes and floppy hats
slow-step, arm in arm,
or stop to watch the setting sun strike silver from the sea.

And down the coast past the train tracks,
sea lions lie like slabs of lard, waiting to give birth,
or wallow into the water to cool off, weightless as butterflies.
And all day and night the sea curls toward land
and smashes, smashes, smashes –
and says *nothing lasts forever...*

Renny Golden

Chief Shabonna's Vision

He fought them, men the color
of clouds. Rock river whispered:

remain, remain. The land's voice:
thrushes, blackbirds, snowy owl.

Its body a tattoo of wild indigo, jewelweed.
Each season told Potawatomi who to become,

how dawn and starlight gave heart
as if the prairie made them,

offered itself, in howl and hoot,
in stillness and white frost.

He fought them with Tecumseh
until his people's blood and theirs

became a stream they could not cross,
could not staunch, could not bear.

He laid down defiance
as a warrior who saw

their dreams and knew
defeat. Shabonna swallowed

the bitter drink of wisdom,
he warned Potawatomi,

warned white settlers,
warned Indians that loss

comes early like snow,
covers rows of the dead.

Ray Johnson

Sweet Old Navajo
(for Mishke, having tapped into Navajo soul)

I play on your land
Sweet Old Navajo with tired joints.
Your cloudy eyes forever see
The other side of what we
Ball players agree
Is the diamond.
Brushing shoulders in the infield,
I thank you for your gracious gaze.
Open vistas on red mesas you've spun
For us, foretelling storm fast approaching.
You've opened your ancestors' door
And I thank you.

Coach Grandfather,
Let me catch you in a double play
Or tag me out at home.
O if Kit Carson ever knew!
Too bad he fell into tortured violence
On the field of manifesting destiny.
So much to gain so much to lose
Before our 7th inning stretch
With nuts and beer.

Sweet Old Navajo,
You send your early morning running son
To our growing city.
Dashing quickly 'round bases
(Barely can deer keep up)
He slides into home
Which once again is his
For this season,

And we thank you
Grandfather.

Sylvia Ramos Cruz

At the Precipice

> *Inspired by cliff dwellings at Walnut Canyon*
> *National Monument, AZ 2017*

Did pre-historic mothers yell
"Keep away from the edge!"
as they scrabbled up canyon walls
like collared lizards
fingers and toes in gritty limestone holes
hoping walnuts plucked along river banks
would not tumble
from baskets tied to narrow waists?

And did those children on ledges far above
listen; scurry back into smoke-stained caves,
or did they lean farther out to watch clouds
gather gray, smell ozone rain?

And was it mothers
who showed them the safest way
to clamber up and down from dwellings
perched where falcons nest?

And did those children dream
soaring high like Icarus
while mothers stayed awake
praying for them
to hail another day?

John Roche

Echoing

of
our drums, bone flutes
voices
against cavern walls

Deep listening
takes place in the dark
or
in sync with
our kindling fire's flickerings

Listen!
We are echoing
Still

(for Pauline Oliveros, 1932-2016)

V.

Dwain Wilder, *Great Sky Spirit*

Dwain Wilder

Great Sky Spirit

Guarding the great Anaconda pit year after year,
the men set to watch had never seen this. Anything
like it. They sent frantic alarms throughout the region,
ran out of their offices waved their arms, shouting,
fired guns, anything to make noise,
anything like it, warding off a living sky.

In vain they tried to haze fear into wildness,
a wildness all alive know deep inside, like this,
as it headed toward the great Anaconda copper pit.
As if its own white sky

filling the horizons, battered by storm,
this great white sky spirit sought refuge
unfrozen refuge in a blizzard,
refuge on open water, anything like it,
and found it
in the poisons of the yawning Anaconda pit.

The company men waved their arms, shouting, fired guns,
anything like it, warning this vast spirit
away from what had been created in these depths.

Ah, but wildness follows its own wisdom, not anything like
the agony of men's regret and remorseful care for their folly.

As if one, the snow geese swirled down into the pit's acid waters
in their tens of thousands, an elegant tornado descending,
and a great sky spirit turned the lake white with its bodies
and dissolved into feathers, beak, claw and remnants of living flesh.

Next morning over that place a high delicate cloud wing rippled,
affording vast refuge for a Great One gone from among us
but not lost.

Larry Goodell

Unwanted

Bring constellations back to your continent.
        But how?
Even the stars have shied away.

The gods – ancient and modern, many faceted and singular –
have turned their backs on Earth they dearly love.
        Come back!
Without your mythologies our stories suffer,
we need the comings and goings of you with us
and the towering cathedrals and dance plazas are echoing
    Vacancy
and Moon, you were so full and large with your man and
        your rabbit –
now you look like a pinprick and it's dark, are you
        shrinking away with your star buddies?

It is dark, even the Sun, my God, you can look at it.
    It's more of a flashlight today and people
are eating in the dark acting like it might be
    their last meal.

What has happened to the Earth: have humans
    turned it into a planet of scorn, the unwanted
        and undesirable in the Cosmos. Must all good things
    shirk us?
What have we done?

Jared Smith

The Storm Upon Us

The winds blow differently
through the hot dry cities this year
and the tombstones that were apartment houses
are wind chimes that no one listens to. The streets
which were going nowhere before now are empty,
children thrown forward through their own windshields.

And the winds blow differently out across the ocean,
weighing more as they drop the human ash they carry
in torrid, whipping hurricanes that breathe out death,
and the hollow skulls of wise men chatter in their rooms
as the winds flicker in and out through lidless eyes.

And the winds blow differently in the mountains too,
carving canyons among the new formed craters
and among the burned grasses of the high plains
and along the eaves of little houses hidden off the grid
where the poorest of us all still hold out and wait
afraid and with their arms about each other wait
for the hard hot rain that will come to them even to them
     before the winds too die out and
no man or animal remarks upon the time at all.

Lauren McLean Ayer

How to Survive the Flood

Stitch a boat from tiny scraps
    the cuff of his old
        flannel shirt
    the wide hem of your
        grandmother's best dress
    the velvet ear of a once-
        stuffed bear

Coat it in wax to protect against weather
    against salt and
        water
    against waves and
        their violence
    against the dark, scaled things
    that circle beneath us

Fill the boat to sustain us on our journey
    with sweets
        from childhood
    with memories and
        stories
    with match and
        tinder

Each night, words
    devour blank pages
Each night, fire
    devours our words
Bathe in the ashes to
    absorb each inflection
Becoming the light
    that will guide us to land

Teresa E. Gallion

Mother

Man is the cruelest animal
and addicted to power and greed.
We actually believe we can control nature.

We drill, we dig, we cut, we frack endlessly
across the earth. Mother continues
to cry from the pain of abuse.

Species are dying, trees are disappearing,
glaciers retreating, water overburdened
with pollution, air becoming dirty.

Hearts continue to beat in denial.
Nature will dump us in the fires of doom.
Here the healing from bad man voodoo begins.

Mountains, meadows and grasslands
hang on, waiting for the good news.
Mother will survive us all.

Ezra Lipschitz

A Serious Laughter

When things are no longer funny,
I find humor to be the best weapon.

The world has lost its collective mind.
(Donald Trump was elected to be
president of the United States.)

But, this is not the first time.
Nor will this be the last—
we know how this works.

We know we're destroying
the planet each time we climb
into the car to go buy condoms.

And I'm talking about the condoms
as much as I am the engine fumes.
All that plastic packaging? Jesus.

But, we also know that babies
are egregiously more expensive
than the condoms we're off to get.

And I'm referring to the environment
as much as I am the empty pocketbook.
All of those disposable diapers? Christ.

We don't have a hell of a lot of time
to figure this stuff out, my friends.

That's why I mixed tequila, rum,
vodka, and gin here in the middle
of a hot, rain-soaked afternoon—
even though I prefer scotch—

a little something to help me
laugh, as I get more serious
about what I'm going to do

to try and help this world
(lost mind and caboodle)

that I've only recently
realized I love,
terribly.

Carlton Holte

Banjaxed

Banjaxed. That was the word we used
when *fucked* or *fucked up*
couldn't be said because of
little ears or other contextual constraints.

Things were not necessarily *FUBAR*:
repair or rescue might be possible.
Much discussion was invested in
what might be done . . .
whether it would be worth it . . .
who should do it and when.

Triage was the heart of it:
banjaxed, FUBAR, or, on occasion,
not as bad as originally suspected.

Then the hard parts:
identifying the party in charge
(logic? your turn, dammit? roshambo?);
testing the limits of stalling;
executing the fix
or calculating the damage
and finding ways to move on.

Michael Peters

ecological josef albers affordable-care-act light event #19
(0% financing on all primal logos survival flashlights™)

death panels
    for grandma?
    for the environment & labor?
    for the earth?

O plug-pulling existential sicknesses
extraterrestrial flyleafs be dam'd
this is the library of damning signs

there's a black out
at bettie beaver's mini-mart
her semantic parking lot
below [look up] & above [look down]
a terrestrial emergency room context

    novalis, gaping at the hubble deep field image
    dante, emerging dirty-knee'd from a sinful earth
    we contemplate angels forming letters
    O sophia   O beatrice   O
    melville, staring at the milky way
    with a knife in his back—

see all that dim'd starry whiteness
on our upturned faces?
uphold your cell camera eyes

there   in the dam of immortal night
turn   to me
you're all aglow with   something?
with   something

hey—
   where *did* you get that logos flashlight?

Leah Zazulyer

Climate Change
                for B. K.

After the Mumbai bombing
my Hindu friend the plant biologist
who lived thirty years in its Chaupati suburb
overlooking the Indian Ocean
began to discuss the problem of evil

remembering when Russian biologists
completely worshipped environmental determinism
but American scientists worshipped genetics…

While some wheat can grow in the north
it won't flower there
just as apples can't flower in the south

each plant has its own periodicity
for flowering initiatives
some more and some less sensitive
to the precise length of a sprouting season

so yes everything is possible
but it is ultimately circumstances
that create good wheat or bad apples

just as it is for people who naturally
self-select the white hot rage
of global warnings, the glacial meltdown of fear,

people whose hearts might still
flower with the apple of sweetness or
instead shrivel into rottenness and
become cadaverous peach pits
or shift and drift like weakened chaff

as each strives to survive
these perilous seasons
of climactic change
by trying to hybridize
their own goodness and evil
into a very very iffy species.

Janet Ruth

Supposition for a Different Age

> —*after Pattiann Rogers' poem, "Supposition"*

Suppose the molecular transformations
happening in the mind during
the act of rising together
resulted in a wave of shouting, clapping
atoms swirling around the earth.
Suppose that wave swelled
in the unification of its intention:
for instance, the expanding ripple
    from a single pebble tossed into a still pool, or
the gradually synchronized tiny blazes
        of chemical flame emanating in response
        to the first firefly's glow.

Suppose rising together, diverse,
had physical properties
and actually perpetuated itself—
    a solid thing.
What if the shape and texture of its being
rose beyond the particular
places of individual risings,
became a permanent music
reverberating in the heavens:
the deep rich *a capella* voices of
Sweet Honey in the Rock—
    round and golden as the rising sun;
pulsing, throbbing drums
in the Oceti Sakowin camp in North Dakota—
    the heartbeats of the Pleiades;
an atomic manifestation,
the musical score for the libretto—
    How wondrous the diversity
    among birds, insects, plants, and humans;
    how particular the greater bird-of-paradise,
    the Madagascan sunset moth, the Venus flytrap,
    the transgender child whose name
    we do not even know.

Suppose rising together diverse,
evolved from our individual beings
by our will and actions,
had its own existence.
What if multi-colored harlequin hues
gathered, combined and recombined
like a kaleidoscope transforming light,
affected the rose tints on the Sandia Mountains
        beneath the setting sun,
or caused a perturbation in the trajectory
        of a yellow-haired meteor flaming
        across our political heavens.

What if rising together diverse
created necessary catalysts
for the tumultuous evolution
of which we dream? Suppose,
for us to rise together,
there was an element of need,
as if a sodium atom sat waiting
for a water molecule with which to ignite
an explosion that would change the world.

Stewart S. Warren

Freed to Feed Our Young

Under the arching maple I am
a nephew studying.
I'm involved in spring, placing a dot
in the center of the sun,
anticipating your arrival.
Renewing breezes bring blooms
though there are less bees this year;
and I am aware of the treacheries
on both coasts, but more so
their aching bodies
and their starving hearts.
Everyone cries under their breath.

Under predawn skies I am
mistress or magi pondering the types
that queens and kings find
only in disturbing dreams.
I step naked to the porch,
but have no interest in spells.
Eloquent stars wheel overhead.

Even now, at this latitude,
Scorpio rising is complete,
stinger and all. She knows
but does not say.
My sigh is her sigh,
my sorrow poised to serve.

I avoid drama, but I'm no fool—
entire species come and go,
human extinctions well known.
O Mother, how many cycles;
how many stranded pelicans,
their wings bound by mud;
how many nights here yearning
on this starlit porch?

VI.

John Roche, *Resist!*

Robbie Sugg

Second Chance

A still life of second chance
lottery tickets fanned out
and pinned down by borrowed
books' precarious balance

and like millennial crows'
offspring next door
moves back in soon after
the workers arrive to
taco truck song stopped short

on the third refrain
to announce the arrival
of sustenance

Tina Carlson

Sorrow and Awe

Let us collect the seed,
the feathery remnants
of hawk feast
the girl's lost limbs
bomb strewn, her fingered
stars that fell in the night,
the horse who nuzzled
a woman's tumor until it dis-
appeared, the meth-laced
holograms of conspiracy,
the brown and black faces of
incarcerations, the threaded
yarn connecting this home
of tree to that bed
of stone; the *swish swish*
of the blood's pulse
its heart clamoring
for some calm.

Veronica Golos

Inverse: A Ghazel
            for my sister

My pale-lit girl, we gathered at dawn; I saw you.
You were a pearl in our mother's see-through anger.

Our father's daughter, skin and shadow; I saw you.
I licked you clean; girded you against disaster.

Two parasols, disoriented light. Dark mouth, but still, I saw you.
She spoke—our mother—crazed to alabaster.

Your voice, its livid red; the morning stung with green—I saw you.
The death of small things, the hunger.

The children that would never, ever see you;
A life ringing in the dark; tinfoil, filled with thunder.

You went alive into the hills, oblivious to what saw you;
only bracken, briar, bone – and no wonder.

Your laced-up mind, your slow montage—anyway, I saw you;
And don't forget, the awful ledge, the One expunger.

Punctual as a cricket, a needle-pointer. Oh sister, I have seen you.
Yet, you allowed me to pass on through, unencumbered.

Your ice patina, your worry and your wreckage; but still, I saw you.
Then, our world, its courage and its faults, was torn, asunder.

Light hurt your eyes. You flaked into scar -- still, I saw you.
You were to swim into color; a child, always younger.

Broken but not extinguished; so still, I saw you.
You called my name, Veronica—True Image? Doppelganger?

Mary Strong Jackson

The Mappist

the mapmaker works across her kitchen table
she untangles the sad from their histories
and worriers from their futures
she ponders the malignant mess
of lies in the Whitest House in the land

she asks, *did no one point to birds or offer backrubs*
when he was four? read stories of Honest Abe?
did his father or mother berate all nuance
from his once tender soul?
does he have a playlist of songwriters singing their songs?

the mappist's lines go deeper than this tangle of lies
she marks memories of millions of American road trips
with glorious detours where sweet songs linger
among roadside apple stands, aging trees, and boulders
more detours for birthings, burials, and road rash

she notes each greasy spoon called "Mom's"
and marks murals of tortilla-making women,
horses pulling plows, blues singers, and butterflies
deeper further multi-layered her lines draw
making mountains   deserts   canyons   prairies

where ashes have been strewn and love made
where specks of egos gaze at stars until
we see our inconsequential selves
but
yet and still

we make our mark!

Janet Eigner

Code Talkers

Before I knew to revere our life's thread,
before the warp of passion had visited our bed,
you, a laboratory Ariadne, wove and unwove the double helices,
questioned what resided where — the clues on each strand.

We dug our passion's bed deep in the yard's loam,
raspberry vines and monkshood, butter
lettuce, and columbine —
your precise patience made fecund.

While untwining the mystery — why
we stayed joined — a biblical span ensued,
ducks chatting over the pickets with passers-by,
our children growing as they wind-winnowed sandbox grains,

until love's skein entwined passion—
DNA transformed on devotion's thread,
a code missing on my helices' natal map,
but spliced in by now and tough as Russian Sage.

Pamela Williams

Even the Engineer Bots from Ghana

So many creatives struggling, these days
to emerge from survival mode.
But deliciously distracted
by the restorative properties
of all that renews in this Spring.
Determined that those warrior tulips
may really bloom as Frankie promised,
if only we watered them.

Shuffling in delight
through the drifts of apricot blossoms,
simple perfection in those petals,
as though drawn by a child.
Offering prayers of deep gratitude
that there are still rain storms, anywhere.
Retaining optimism that we may yet
restore this planet
to some of its former magic.
I listen raptly to the latest belief
in radionics.

An abundance of scammers and scoundrels
afoot, this week,
clueless of the joy in apricot blossoms,
and threatening to trammel on the cracked armor
of the prevailing courage.

Overlaid on this tapestry of life,
our kids continue to leave with what
can only be hope for
just another day at school.
Their emerging wisdom
beckoning a fresh path
for all our survival.

Robert E. McDonough

Timothy Caughman in California

He staggered off the bus with cramps, and for
forever, that was all there was. No time
to part friends from the people on the bus
or to think that he'd known Shari Headley would
not meet him. He got his bag and stood tall
as he could, stretched out the cramps until
walking at least hurt less than standing, then
less some more, and then he was back in time
and there were palm trees and more sun than
there'd ever been in Manhattan,
and everything was California.

He began to walk for real. Without cramps
his legs still worked, and he had thousands
of miles of sitting to walk off. "Winter"
here, too, but only California winter.
He was glad he'd stuffed his coat into his bag.
He saw a newspaper headline about
some racial killing in NY, and was sad
for a minute, but he was here to enjoy.
He knew where to find a room, and his phone map
would take him past a piece of street art
he'd come all this way to see: "Abraham
Obama," Barack's face inside Lincoln's
hair and beard. Then he'd find a Carl's, Jr.
for food, and tomorrow Grauman's Chinese Theatre.

Note: *According to The New York Times, Timothy Caughman, a sixty-six-year-old black man, was murdered in Manhattan on March 20, 2017, allegedly by a twenty-eight-year-old white supremacist, who had travelled from Baltimore to kill Black men. The alleged murderer is said to have expressed regret that he didn't choose a younger victim. Timothy Caughman had wished on Twitter that he might someday visit California. As far I know, President Trump has said nothing on Twitter or elsewhere about Mr. Caughman's death.*

Alecia Lutrario

Girl Made of Hazards

Caution signs and trails closed
Water roaring over impulses
I didn't drive this far to turn away

A state park called stony brook
A childhood home to be barred from
due to "hazardous conditions"

I climbed over the "Do-Not-Enter" gate

Walked with bare feet in freezing water
in conditions the sign called hazardous
felt alive for the first time in weeks

Climbed over rocks and pondered over
the uncertainty of being here alone
for the first time

Over the feeling of being alone
but for once not scared

Craving isolation as I watched the sun shine
over the waterfall I used to swim in
my Winnie the Pooh bathing suit
and water shoes

I realize that the only hazardous thing
in this park
is me

Gary Brower

Escaping the End of the World

> *The survival of the human race depends on
> its ability to find new homes elsewhere in the
> universe because there's an increasing risk
> that a disaster will destroy the Earth.*
> —Stephen Hawking AP news conference (6/13/06).
>
> *Rocket Summer, the words passed among
> the people ... Rocket Summer.*
> —Ray Bradbury, *The Martian Chronicles.*
>
> *When everyone goes to other planets, I will stay in the
> abandoned city ... walk the rusted rails,
> ...listen to records of 1930s songs, never caring
> to look at the infinite roads traced by rockets in space.*
> —Jorge Teillier, *When Everyone goes.*

I opened the car door of memory,
traveled roads even ghosts
no longer haunt.

As I drove back from
the precipice called Omega,
in a turquoise blue and white,
1956 Chevy sedan from my past
seemg no one,
I realized our continual
non-stop wars and ecocide
might have finally brought us
to the end we thought would never come.

We've become too reptilian,
I thought,
scales on our eyes,
like humanosaurs,
clawing our way
to oblivion.

I pulled up to an old railroad crossing,
realized there was no reason to stop,
even though red lights were flashing
from an ancient warning signal, its bell clanging
as if calling machines to prayer.

I started to cross the rusted rails,
but out of nowhere,
a train with no engineer suddenly roared by,
the whoosh of its wake moving toward blinding light,
till the caboose faded from view,
a ghost named Future in the empty bar-car
ordering drinks of dust,
as the machine plunged over a broken tressel
in the planet of my head.

Links of the Great Chain of Being
were melting down, like borders of real and unreal,
the mirage of current history a Daliesque landscape
fading into impossible incarnations of deja vu
we had never seen before.

I missed the emotional part of Armageddon,
the erasure of cartoon religions
that couldn't produce a messiah to save the world
after the public was told the "nuclear option" that was used
would bring deathly drops of radiation rain
while at the same time,
there was no doubt a meteor
would kiss the earth with its apocalips.

As the Great Circle of Death moved closer,
panicked crowds locked
into the last dome of the take-off area
heard those left outside
invoking names of Rodan and Megalon or Godzilla
referred to in the chapter of New Revelations
from the Revised Book of the Good Life.

I looked down from the cockpit
like a stuffed animal in my ill-fitting spacesuit,
flashed on the kaleidoscope of my past
which recreated fragments of dreams
that continually changed into nightmares

as I heard an ethereal voice say:
"two minutes to lift-off,"
the end of the countdown echoing
in my helmet: "zero, zero, zero, zero."

I shook off the calming injection,
kept talking into my memo-pod,
as the rocket suddenly exploded
toward a distant orbit-road,
moved to puncture gravity before the death-rain,
ahead of the meteor's arrival,
escape the final impact that would pull us back
to the end of the world,
as we tried to outrun our own stupidity
leave behind our soon-to-be cinder of galactic garbage,
head for a planet-colony we hoped still there,
swinging on our airship trapeze
in the big-tent circus of constellations,
looking for a moon of Jupiter named Mozart,
listening to Holtz's "The Planets,"
the shining Music of the Spheres,
down to the Zodiac's last desperate notes,
waiting for the future of History
to explode like a train
colliding with light
at the end
of the world.

Craig Czury

Wind Hurling Stones

There are stones in the rain that knock us down

Wind hurling stones that rip straight through our coats
as if our coats were filled with nothing but air

Our coats are not filled with nothing but air
I can show you the sores

And it's with our great love for coats
(and the flesh we survive)
that we've chosen your doorstoop
your heavy sheets of cardboard
your alley behind the dumpster to sprawl out and live

Craig Czury

Above the Back Alley

two 2nd floor windows with a door between them
but there's no staircase
the one I'm looking for lives here
and as I walk around to the front *[click]*
each evening before soup at the Mission we loved to sing
like men abandoned to the deathship of salvation
all those words we knew be heart
because if the henchmen of Jesus caught us sleeping
they'd throw us back out
sometimes I could count lice shinny up the strands of hair
in front of me
and though I've only been in jail twice
looking for you and remembering this
like some hunger from the past left to be fed all over
it was cold damn cold out there that one night
with a mist that cuts through no matter how many layers
and the mattresses thrown out on the hotel stoops soaking wet
maybe it's memory
or for memory and warmth those two winos meshed their beards
and heavy coats at the bellies clutching each other
against a doorway in a passionate kiss
or to just make themselves feel beautiful
the way (poets say) the mind lets go
door with no staircase
not like this looking for you and seeing me at the same time

Georgia Santa Maria

Arizona Dogs

The old dogs looked for shade,
bedeviled the weeping cypress
circling her roots three times
bit at the sway of her branches.
An Arizona dog takes
what shade he can get
free of a prickly pear cactus
the phone pole like saguaro
peopled with would-be
vermin along its axis.
A prayer for rain unanswered,
even rag-weed wilts in this heat.
This drought-wise tree takes heed,
stays light as lace, and breathes.

Herb Kauderer

Surviving Low Tide

The first hundred days
will blow away
into the frozen graveyard
of winters past.
The roller coaster
ride of stress
will continue
to surprise and agitate.
We will continue
to suffer the ride
despite our indigestion.
Persevere.
As surely as the tide
goes out
the tide returns.

Dianne Borsenik

Tides

> *"When they go low, we go high."*
> —Michelle Obama

Beginnings, almost imperceptible.
      Neap tide, right angled astronomy,
  barely a ripple
           to expose the pulling away....

Gradually, a stronger undertow
      as solar and lunar gravities diverge.
  A more insistent tugging,
        a more insistent return,

conchitic signatures inscribed
      and erased, a fresh epistle each time.
  Without the power
        of geometry to slow

the surge, expansion of range,
      spring tide blurring practiced certainty
  into fuzzy aftermath.

           Now,
      here, new ribbons form

and coalesce on shifting shores.
      Neap tides swell into a rising, becoming.
  Breakers of change:
        struggle, renunciation;

acquiescence refused,
      heterogeneity embraced. At the crest,
  one wave merged
        from many, resolute.

Deimos, stripped of the power
      to scream, liturgy denied. Gravities
  diverge.
        Now, here,
           a spring tide, going high.

Martha Deed

After Whitman

Sea surges against the dunes of Truro, the sand shark swims beside
    the kayak drifting empty on the swells of Cape Cod Bay;
Wind lifts the cap off the head of the child who looks for silver
    dollars and clams on the beach;
Old woman watches skin of her arms and belly and buttocks unravel;

Union soldiers crowd the decks of the hospital ship;
one writes to his cousin on Long Island,
"I think I shall survive so don't be alarmed,"
letter in the yellowed envelope, banded in black,
    preserved in the cousin's desk 'til found a century hence.

These are the marks of time but do not tell the meaning,
These are not the tides of the Pacific, the Indian, the seas of Antarctica,
These are not the falling ice of the polar caps, or the Brown Booby
    stranded on the breakwater rocks of Buffalo.

See not death settle upon the shark in shallow waters,
the child dying soon of invisible disease,
the old woman sick in her bed,
the world grown tired of survival,
the wounded soldier in his cot,
the Southern bird dying of ice.

I feel the chill wind against my cheeks;
I hear the gulls fighting for fish;
I taste the misted waters of Niagara;
I move with the ash trees and the emerald ash borers
    who move with them also.

Brave the living with courage to see!
Brave the dead of land and sea!
Brave the man who watches the planets, the asteroid passing the moon;
Blessed the woman whose sight connects the dust, the bees, the skies,
    the wretched men, the gods.

For the sea is not life and war is not death and the soldier writing letters
    cannot disappear with the clams or the child playing on the sand;
For I see all of them and the universe is known to me also and the poet
    who writes his songs and sings his lines is all that is known to me.

Colleen Powderly

What Would Walt Whitman Do?

He'd put his foot on the rail,
hoist a glass to the going,
toast his friend's life.
*The best of men! Always
moving! Always talking!
Always doing!* Then clap
him on the back,
smile, say *Congrats!*

Walk him to the station,
see him to the train, stare hard
at people and buildings, avoid
windows and his face.
He'd salute the receding Pullman,
glad for steam clouding his eyes.
Then stride the miles to Mother's,
howl a yawp to say goodbye.

Veronica Golos

Rain Song
—*after Badr Shakir al Sayyab*

...it's raining thick gray New York rain--rain that fills the gutters that soaks my coat
seeps down the back of my neck and when I finally climb on the bus the rain is steam

rising off my shoulders, the bus drive has his hands on the large wheel, is urging the huge
animal of the bus forward, is stroking the wheel   whispering or praying as we make

our way through the pouring, the hoe and screech of traffic muted, we are all swaying
in a steaming bus the light begins its change from red to green---look

at the passengers, our faces are beginning to blur, there is a crying rising, as if
we are being filled with rain, rain is tapping on our organs, is filling

the crevices of our lungs, liver, heart, heads, our craniums, the eight bones
of the wrist, our particular fingernails; the rain outside is carrying on, is almost wild,

pouring itself into the world, wordless and trouble, and we who are almost sheltered
in this steam and fog and huffing bus, the earth in us is rising, the rain is wearing us

down to humid dirt, as if we could begin again, perhaps we could change,
become someone else, empty our pockets, change

our clothes, hair, the color of our skin, become a man, woman, grow to childhood
again, or age so quickly our bones would be made of light and we would glide

down the rain-soaked streets, the gleam of rain still on the tar, on the huge billboards,
the streetlights surrounded with halo, night coming on, and the stars and moon

would be bright and clean and pure and there would be no war, and the hungry
would be fed, and the children loved, as we would be loved, and oh,

life is good and will be different, won't it, won't it, when we step off the bus in the rain.

Mark Granier

The Whew

is the animal that whistle-climbs
out of our lungs, our chest,
our shoulders, and all the rest

to stand shivering its invisible limbs
deliciously, allowing us see through
what we survived into:

our shadow's shadow
taking one breath, then another, now ——

Martha Treichler

Survival

Survival is only the beginning,
life starts after that.

When you say, "I survived!"
that is good
but not good enough.

Survival is only the beginning,
then we must
gather our tools
and get to work.

Bios

Sam Abrams (28), born in Brooklyn, was a Fulbright Professor at the University of Athens and is Professor Emeritus at Rochester Institute of Technology. In the 1960s, he taught at the St. Mark's Poetry Project and was a member of Stone Academy, an organic farming commune in Enfield, NH. He has authored *The Neglected Whitman*, *The Old Pothead Poems*, and *The Post-American Cultural Congress: Selected Poems*. >Sam shoots from the hip.

Lydia Andrews (9) is a student at the University of New Mexico. She is currently pursuing a Bachelor's degree in Psychology, with a minor in English. In 2016, she began volunteering at Agora Crisis Center. Her poetry has appeared in the *Fixed and Free Anthology* and in *Leonardo*, a literary journal published by Central New Mexico Community College.

H. Marie Aragón (145) lives and writes in Eldorado, New Mexico, where she found gold in the writing community. Aragon's poetry has been published in numerous journals and anthologies. In 2014 her work was presented as a mini-feature in the *Malpaís Review*. In 2015 she won the Lummox Poetry Prize, leading to a chapbook: *When Desert Willows Speak*. Recently, her poems were published in *Live Santa Fe 's Anthology # 5*.

Steve Ausherman (13) is a poet, painter and photographer who resides in New Mexico. He has been thrice nominated for the Pushcart Prize in poetry and has had two chapbooks of his poetry published entitled *Creek Bed Blue* and *Marking the Bend* (both published by Encircle Publications).

Lauren McLean Ayer (158, 190) is a San Francisco-grown poet and writer who moved to Santa Fe to find peace in the desert. When not sitting in coffee shops trying to write, she likes to design and make art quilts based on super powers. Her poems have appeared in *Gargoyle Magazine*, *Santa Fe one heart*, *Adobe Walls*, and online.

Dick Bakken (113), born 1941, grew up in Montana/Washington/Oregon, but since 1980 has lived a mile high in Bisbee, AZ. Jump hard from his front porch and you'll land in Sonora, Mexico. His 50-year retrospective, *The Whiskey Epiphanies: Selected Poems 1963-2013*, can be ordered at www.pleasureboatstudio.com. Bakken's *Greatest Hits 1967-2002* (Pudding House) is now available only from dickbakken@yahoo.com

Megan Baldrige (33) is a retired English teacher, gardener, Japanophile, museum-docenting, garden-loving mom of four grown children, who has lived in Connecticut half her life, and Cedar Crest and Albuquerque the better half of her life.

Currently working on his second volume of poetry, *Medicine*, **John Berry** (38) writes from his Winchester VA home with his beloved wife, Brenda, and their constant yorkie companions, Molly and Lily. When not engaged in his profession as a woodworker and cabinet-maker, John hosts a monthly poetry open-mic and an internet poetry show, The Sock Drawer Poetry Series, on www.winlifetv.com

Joanne Bodin Ph.D. (68, 126) is an award-winning author and poet. Her book of poetry *Piggybacked* was a finalist in the New Mexico Book Awards. Her novel *Walking Fish* won the NM Book Award and the International Book Award in gay/lesbian fiction. *Orchid of the Night* was a finalist for the Eric Hoffer Award and the NM Press Women Communication Award, and won the NM Book Award in LGBT fiction.

Dianne Borsenik (216) is active in the northern Ohio poetry scene and Midwest reading circuit. Her poems have appeared in *Chiron Review, Rosebud, Slipstream, The Offbeat*, and others. Lit Youngstown put her poem "Disco" on their tee shirts, which makes her feel like a rock star. Find her at www.dianneborsenik.com.

Rich Boucher's poems (36) have appeared in *Gargoyle, The Nervous Breakdown, Apeiron Review, The Mas Tequila Review, In Between Hangovers, Menacing Hedge*, and *Cultural Weekly*, among others. From the summer of 2016 to the spring of 2017, he served as the Associate Editor and Weekly Poem Curator at *Elbow Room Magazine*.

Kate Bremer (131, 132) lives in the rocky hill country of Central Texas with cats, dogs, burros and a horse. She loves to host writing and drumming circles with the beautiful and perceptive herd to offer people an experience of nature, creativity, and fellowship. Her website is www.foresthorse.com

Summer Brenner (75) is the author of crime fiction, award-winning YA novels, literary short stories, and the occasional essay, including a chapter in Rebecca Solnit's *Infinite City*.

G.L. Brower (209) has published six books of poetry and four CDs. He is the Editor of *Malpais Review*, a past director of the Duende Poetry Series of Placitas, NM, has taught at Kansas, UNM, USC, UCLA, UCSD, and in Spain and Mexico. He has also been a journalist (Spanish and English), and directed programs for Mexican migrant workers.

Michele Brown (121) writes about whatever comes to notice in the path of her day. When not writing, she dreams of food without poison, metal- and wood-working, all manner of drawn and written art, as well as finding edible plants in her garden in the Genesee River Watershed.

Tony Brown (65) is from Worcester MA. A six-time Pushcart Prize nominee, he fronts the poetry and music band The Duende Project. His latest chapbook is *In the Embers*, from Tired Hearts Press (2016).

Lauren Camp (45, 91) is the author of three books, including *One Hundred Hungers* (Tupelo Press), finalist for the Arab American Book Award and winner of the Dorset Prize. Her poems have appeared in *Slice, Love's Executive Order, Boston Review, Poetry International,* and the Poem-a-Day series from The Academy of American Poets. Her honors include a Black Earth Institute Fellowship and the opportunity to be Visiting Scholar for the Mayo Clinic. She lives and teaches in New Mexico. www.laurencamp.com

Tina Carlson (202) is a poet and a psychiatric nurse practitioner at Albuquerque Healthcare for the Homeless. Her book *Ground, Wind, This Body* was published by UNM Press in 2017.

Deborah Coy (21, 165) has published three books and has been published in several anthologies and online poetry publications. She was an editor for the anthology, *La Llorona*, published by Beatlick Press, which won the New Mexico/Arizona Book Awards for Anthology in 2013.

Craig Czury (212, 213) lives between Albania, Lithuania and N.E. Pennsylvania. Author of *Thumb Notes Almanac: Hitchhiking the Marcellus Shale*, his new book, *Fifteen Stones*, is a collection of prose poems from Italy, Chile, and the spaces between. craigczury.com

Martha Deed (217) longs to spit fire but writes poems instead. Climate Change (Foothills Publishing, 2014) The Last Collaboration (Furtherfield, 2012). Edited Millie Niss's poetry collection, City Bird (BlazeVox, 2010). Several chapbooks. Her poems appear in anthologies, many poetry journals. Blogs on http://sporkworld.tumblr.com/

During the day, **Steven Deridder** (47, 85) tutors reading, writing and the SAT. At night, he is a poet with a passion for photography, currently on vacation from both to finish his first sci-fi novel. His work has most recently been published in *Enzigam, Pencil Marks,* and *Mo' Joe: The Joe the Poet Anthology*.

Orin Domenico (175) lives in Utica, NY where he and his wife, Kim, have for 16 years run the Cafe Domenico and for 12 years, The Other Side, a non-profit public forum and gallery dedicated to anarchy and the arts. His chapbook, *And Louder Sing: Selected Poems (1997-2013)*, was published by Black Rabbit Press, which publishes the Utica literary quarterly *Doubly Mad*.

Arthur O. DuBois (64) is a socially conscious professional social worker. He currently works as a psychotherapist and with the public defenders' office. He has been married to Susan for thirty years, and has two sons and one daughter. He intermittently writes poetry, but often just ruminates.

Mary Dudley (18, 138) received a master's degree in English from SUNY/Stony Brook before moving to Albuquerque, New Mexico, where she earned a Ph.D. in child development across cultures. She has worked with young children and their families for many years. Her poetry has appeared in numerous publications.

Nicolas Eckerson (73, 92) is an aspiring poet from Rochester, NY and a graduate of RIT, where he worked on the staff of *Signatures Magazine* and won a Kearse Award for Creative Writing. He has read at the Black Mountain North Symposium, Rochester Fringe Festival, Imagine RIT Fest, Cloudburst, Gallery r, and Writers & Books, and has been published in *Big Bridge*, *Canto*, and several anthologies.

Jesse Ehrenberg (103) came to New Mexico from New York in the early 70s. He started writing poetry as a teenager and still finds inspiration in the power of words. His poems have appeared in local anthologies. His recent poetry book *"Surprise!"* won awards in both the New Mexico and National Press Women's 2018 Communications contests. It's available from FootHills Publishing.

Janet Eigner's (139, 205) *What Lasts is the Breath* (2013) was a winner in the AZ-NM Book Awards 2013 and a finalist in the NM Newspaper Women Contest, 2015. She was a Poetry Foundation Poet, was on American Life in Poetry, and has published dance articles and reviews. Forthcoming, a collection documenting 12 backpack trips over four decades into the Grand Canyon.

Stephen Ellis (99) was born in another time and place. No college, no high school. Played football in Syria, Iran and Serbia. Began writing 1990. Edited from US, 26 issues of poetry magazine *:that:* (1992-1994), and from Israel, Jordan and US, 105 folded broadsides and 26 fascicles published under Oasis Press imprint (1995-2005). Publication of his own work has been sporadic and sparse, but can be viewed at http://proposia.blogspot.com

Alexis Rhone Fancher (160) is the author of *How I Lost My Virginity To Michael Cohen and other heart stab poems* (2014), *State of Grace: The Joshua Elegies* (2015), *Enter Here* (2017), and *Junkie Wife* (2018). Her photos are published worldwide. A multiple Pushcart Prize and Best of the Net nominee, Alexis is poetry editor of *Cultural Weekly*. www.alexisrhonefancher.com

Mark Fleisher (119) is the author of three poetry collections, *Moments of Time, Intersections: Poems from the Crossroads,* and *Reflections: Soundings from the Deep.* He also collaborated with Dante Berry on *Obituaries of the Living.* The Albuquerque resident earned a journalism degree from Ohio University and served in Vietnam with the U.S. Air Force.

Michael C. Ford (52) is credited with over 28 volumes of print documents, as well as approx. 60 spoken word tracks. His debut vinyl received a Grammy nomination in 1986 and his *Selected Poems* earned a Pulitzer nomination in 1998. Hen House Studios markets his CD project *Look Each Other in the Ears* [2014], featuring a stellar band of musicians, including surviving members of a 1960s theatre rock quartet most of you will remember as The Doors.

Teresa E. Gallion (191) has been published in numerous journals and anthologies. She has two CDs, *On the Wings of the Wind* and *Poems from Chasing Light,* and three books: *Walking Sacred Ground, Contemplation in the High Desert and Chasing Light.* The latter was a finalist in the 2013 NM/AZ Book Awards. You may preview her work at: http://bit.ly/1aIVPNq or http://bit.ly/13IMLGh

Renny Golden (181) is a writer, professor emerita, poet, and social justice activist. Her books reflect concerns for those made voiceless or marginalized. "I grew up in Chicago on the Southeast side influenced by an Irish grandfather who co-founded Local 399 (originally the 'Micks' who shoveled coal into furnaces) and an Irish grandmother who was a *seanchai* (story-teller)."

Veronica Golos (203, 219) is the author of three award-winning books: *A Bell Buried Deep* (Story Line Press; Nicholas Roerich Poetry Prize); *Vocabulary of Silence* (Red Hen Press; New Mexico Poetry Prize); and *Rootwork* (3: A Taos Press). She is Co-Editor of the *Taos Journal of International Poetry & Art*; former Poetry Editor, *Journal of Feminist Studies in Religion*; and core faculty for *Tupelo Press Writing Conference.*

Vincent F. A. Golphin (71) teaches and writes in Central Florida. His most recent book, *Grandma Found a Gecko,* an early reader, was published in 2016. In 2012, FootHills Publishing released *Ten Stories Down,* poems based on his experiences in Beijing, China, and, in 2006, *Like A Dry Land: A Soul's Journey through the Middle East,* inspired by a 2003 visit to Jordan.

Manuel González (116) is City of Albuquerque Poet Laureate 2016-2018. Manuel began his career in Poetry Slam and now teaches workshops on self-expression through poetry in schools, youth treatment facilities, and youth detention centers. Manuel is also creator and organizer of Burque's "Louder Than a Bomba" Youth Slam.

Sarita Sol González (22) is a 13-year-old performance poet from Albuquerque. Sarita has been published in various poetry anthologies and in 2016 published *Burquenita* (Swimming With Elephants Publications). In April 2016, Sarita had the honor of being asked by then US Poet Laureate, Juan Felipe Herrera, to perform with him at the Library of Congress in Washington DC. Sarita is currently working on her next book of poetry, due out later this year.

Larry Goodell (26, 188) is a poet of performance and page, raconteur of earth's debacle from human greed, satirist of government secrecy and local real estate development, pianist, song-writer, playwright, performance poetry organizer, native of Roswell (1935) and resident of Placitas since 1963, a life-long organic gardener and founder of duende press. See www.larrygoodell.com/ and www.granarybooks.com/collections/goodell/

Mark Granier's poems (127, 220) have appeared in numerous outlets in Ireland and the UK over the years, and also on the *Daily Poem* and *Verse Daily* websites. Prizes and awards include the Vincent Buckley Poetry Prize, four Arts Council bursaries and two Patrick and Katherine Kavanagh Fellowships. His fifth collection, *Ghostlight: New & Selected Poems*, was published by Salmon Poetry in May 2017.

Kenneth P. Gurney (54, 67) lives in Albuquerque, NM, USA with his beloved Dianne. His latest collection of poems is *Layover* (2018). His personal blog is at umflop.com.

Sheryl Guterl (98), retired teacher and elementary school counselor, mother of six and grandmother of seven, now lives in Albuquerque. Her poems have appeared online through Teachers and Writers Collaborative and in the inaugural edition of Months to Years. When not traveling, she can be found reading, hiking, docenting at the Albuquerque Museum, tutoring ESL, or singing. She is enchanted with life in Albuquerque.

Mina Hatami (143) is an Iranian American writer whose poems tell a story of tension along the continuum of doubt certitude love and hate. She is active with the Just Poets organization in Rochester, NY.

Ceinwen E. Cariad Haydon's (70) stories have been published on *Fiction on the Web, Literally Stories, StepAway* and *Alliterati*. Her poems are published in *Poems to Survive In, Writers Against Prejudice, Trumped, Hers, Water,* and *I am not a Silent Poet*. She graduated from Newcastle University, UK, in 2017 with an MA in Creative Writing

Wendy Heath (137) is an American artist and poet living in England. Her chapbook *Radio Lent* is published by the Knives Forks and Spoons Press.

William Heyen (171, 172) lives in Brockport, New York. He is the author of more than thirty books, including *Noise in the Trees*, an ALA Notable Book for 1975, *Crazy Horse in Stillness*, winner of 1997's Small Press Book Award for Poetry, and *Shoah Train: Poems*, a Finalist for the 2004 National Book Award. His most recent book is *The Candle: Poems of Our 20th Century Holocausts* (Etruscan Press). wheyen@rochester.rr.com

Kevin Higgins (96) teaches Creative Writing at Galway Technical Institute and is Creative Writing Director for NUI Galway Summer School. His poetry is discussed in *The Cambridge Introduction to Modern Irish Poetry* and featured in the noteworthy anthology *Identity Parade —New British and Irish Poets* (Bloodaxe, 2010). *Stinging Fly* magazine calls Kevin, "likely the most read living poet in Ireland." He has published five collections of poetry with Salmon Press, most recently *Song of Songs 2.0: New & Selected Poems* (2017).

Carlton Holte (193). Born in the tundra before color TV. Grew up playing under bridges, along creeks, in cornfields. Went to lots of school, then gigs as teacher, writer, editor, and less wordy things. Recently introduced to red, green, and Christmas–color, heat, and fun on the same plate! Likes to write about love, trees, and blue water, and to discover good places to eat.

Catherine Iselin (94) lives in Amherst, Massachusetts, where she currently teaches piano and piano improvisation in her private studio. She has also worked as a French teacher and translator ever since moving here from her native Switzerland. Back in 2004, Catherine started writing poetry with Pat Schneider's Amherst Writers and Artists' Workshop.

Mary Strong Jackson's work (69, 204) has appeared in journals and anthologies in the US and England. Her chapbooks include *The Never-Ending Poem, Witnesses, No Buried Dogs, Between Door and Frame*, and *Clippings*. Read more at strongjacksonpoet.wordpress.com. Mary recently returned to the high desert where she lives near Otowi Bridge in New Mexico.

Raymond Warren Johnson (156, 182) hails from Milwaukee where he earned a degree in Italian and Spanish at UWM. He's a 70-year-old softball player with a .750 batting average who woodworks, makes cabinets, trims trees. Proud father of Nataniel Tzvi, public defender in the East Bay. He can ride a horse and meditate, but not at the same time. He likes metaphor.

Kitty Jospé (41, 77) completed her MFA in poetry at Pacific University in 2009 and has published 5 books. The latest is *Twilight Venus* (FootHills Publishing, 2018). Her poems appear in *Nimrod, Grasslimbs, Poetrybay, Centrifugal Eye, Vehicle* and multiple anthologies. For her, poetry is an effective art for channeling words to carry meanings that strike at the heart.

Kathamann (42, 55) is a returned Peace Corps Volunteer/Afghanistan and a retired registered nurse. She has been active in the Santa Fe arts community for 30 years, exhibiting in juried, group and solo exhibits (kathamann.com). Her poems have occasionally been published in local and regional anthologies.

Herb Kauderer (43, 215) is an associate professor of English at Hilbert College and lives near the US border of Canada. In fact, he is married to a Canadian, proving that borders are not nearly so dividing as some would have us believe.

Mary Ellen Kelly (24) enjoys her retirement from community college teaching through spending time with family and friends, writing, photography, and volunteering. Writing poetry to raise funds for the Center for New Americans, the organization in her Massachusetts community that welcomes immigrants, gave her a way to shout out against post-election despair and to connect with the hope inherent in creative acts.

David Landrey (174) spent 38 years teaching literature, 35 of them at Buffalo State College. For three of those years he taught in Turkey. He studied briefly with Charles Olson at SUNY Buffalo. He is the author of *Intermezzi to Divorce Poems and Dinner Table Scenes*, from Jensen/Daniels. *Consciousness Suite* was published by Spuyten Duyvil. Destitute Press has published a selection of his poems.

John Landry (53, 111) was born in New Bedford, Massachusetts, where he served as poet laureate. He read his work at the Library of Congress at the invitation of Gwendolyn Brooks. His book *who will prune the plum tree when i'm gone* was published in Chile by Editorial Cuneta. A subsequent volume, *anthropocene debris*, will appear in Chile in 2018, in addition to a "selected poems" from Lithic Press in CO. He served as Guest Editor for the *Cape Cod Poetry Review* 4/5 Summer 2018. He resides in Albuquerque.

Mary Elizabeth Lang (15) is a retired college instructor living in Connecticut. She earned her MFA from Bennington College Writing Seminars. Her poems have appeared in several anthologies and journals, including *Ekphrasis, The Prose Poem*, and *Comstock Review*. Her first full-length book of poetry was *Under Red Cedars* (2008); her latest chapbook is *Permanent Guests* (2018).

Gayle Lauradunn's (62, 93) collection *Reaching for Air* was named a Finalist by the Texas Institute of Letters for the Best First Book of Poetry. A second collection, *All the Wild and Holy: A Life of Eunice Williams 1696-1785*, recently appeared from FootHills Publishing. A pocket chapbook, *Duncan Canal, Alaska*, is available from Grandma Moses Press. Her life has been devoted to social justice activism, and she still hopes it has not been in vain.

Poet and painter **Alice Lee** (48) has been published and had solo art shows nationally and internationally. Her poetry has appeared in *Calyx, Adobe Walls, New Mexico Poetry Review*, and others. Her latest publication is *Sometimes She Talks to Crows: Poems by Alice Lee* (Kelsay Books, 2018).

Lyn Lifshin (159) has published over 130 books and chapbooks including 3 from Black Sparrow Press: *Cold Comfort, Before it's Light*, and *Another Woman who Looks Like Me*. Recent books include *Secretariat; Knife Edge & Absinthe; Malala; A Girl Goes into the Woods; Femme Eternal;* and *Little Dancer: the Degas Poems*. She edited 3 anthologies: *Tangled vines, Lips Unsealed; Ariadne's Thread*. Her web: www: lynlifshin.com

Jane Lipman's (149) first book, *On the Back Porch of the Moon*, Black Swan Editions, won the 2013 NM/AZ Book Award and a NM Press Women's Award. Her chapbooks, *The Rapture of Tulips* and *White Crow's Secret Life*, were finalists for NM Book Awards in 2009 and 2010. She founded and directed Taos Institute, sponsoring workshops by Robert Bly, Gioia Timpanelli, Joseph Campbell, Paul Winter, and others.

Ezra Lipschitz (128, 192) was born in 1955, then mostly raised, in Colma, California. He completed a degree in English at UC Davis, but doesn't recall getting his diploma. His first book, *I Shouldn't Say…*, appeared in 2017 from Mezcalita Press, LLC.

Alecia Lutrario (170, 208) is a Senior at Rochester Institute of Technology, where she has been literary editor for the campus literary & art magazine *Signatures*, a member of the public relations student society of America (PRSSA), and also participated in the CUPSI national slam competition.

Jennifer Maloney (150) started writing poetry, songs and stories when she was a child. She is also a singer (performing with her husband and with an as-yet-unnamed band), and learning to dance burlesque! She is currently President of the Just Poets organization in Rochester, NY.

Freya Manfred's (97, 180) sixth collection of poetry, *Swimming with a Hundred Year Old Snapping Turtle*, won the 2009 Midwest Bookseller's Choice Award. Her eighth collection is *Speak, Mother*, also from Red Dragonfly Press. A longtime Midwesterner who has lived on both coasts, her poetry has appeared in over 100 reviews and magazines and over 40 anthologies. Her memoir, *Frederick Manfred: A Daughter Remembers*, was nominated for a Minnesota Book Award and an Iowa Historical Society Award.

Kate Marco (157) has been writing poetry and prose since she learned to put pen to paper. In 1976, Seven Stars published a small book of her poems, *Through The Changes, Gently* (under the name Kathleen Keller), which reached #4 on the small press bestseller list. Kate has published in newspapers and poetry journals for several decades. She was poetry editor for *Artlines* magazine in Taos, New Mexico.

Demetria Martinez (163) is an Albuquerque writer and activist who believes that no human being is illegal. Among her books are *Breathing Between the Lines* (poetry, U. Arizona), *Mother Tongue* (novel, Ballantine), *The Block Captain's Daughter* (short stories, U. Oklahoma) *Confessions of a Berlitz Tape Chicana* (essays, U. Oklahoma). She is the currently working on a new book of short stories; the working title is *Dark Notes*.

Robert E. McDonough (207) taught composition and English and American literature for more than forty years at Cuyahoga Community College in Cleveland. He has published *No Other World* (poems) from the Cleveland State University Poetry Center and *Greatest Hits* (a chapbook of poems) from Pudding House, as well as numerous poems in magazines and anthologies.

Mary McGinnis (134, 167) has been writing and living in New Mexico since 1972. Having the disability of blindness all her life challenged her to have a career. Besides appearing in over 70 magazines and anthologies, she has published three full-length collections: *Listening for Cactus* (1996), *October Again* (2008), and *See with Your Whole Body* (2016). She was the first recipient of the Gratitude Award from the NM Literary Arts Board in 2009.

Karla Linn Merrifield (51, 153), a National Park Artist-in-Residence, has 12 books to her credit; the newest is *Bunchberries, More Poems of Canada*. She is assistant editor and book reviewer for *The Centrifugal Eye*. Give her name a Google to read more and visit her at http://karlalinn.blogspot.com

Merimee Moffitt (8, 125) writes to make sense of things, to investigate, to rant, to emote, to use a voice once silenced. Feminism is a no-brainer, she says, and losing the chance to have a woman president is the biggest disappointment ever. She has published four books: *Making Little Edens; Free Love, Free Fall* (a memoir); *Berlin Poems and Photographs* (co-authored with Georgia Santa Maria); and *Notes on Serenity*, a book about loving and surviving with an addicted child. She has four kids, six grandkids, a kind and patient husband, and one little dog named Clyde.

David Morse's poetry (35, 84) has appeared in *California Quarterly, Crab Creek Review, Friends Journal, The Kerf (nominated for a Pushcart Prize), Potomac Review,* and elsewhere. He is the author of a novel, *The Iron Bridge* (Harcourt Brace). His essays have appeared in *Esquire, The Nation,* and *The New York Times Magazine.* David lives in rural Connecticut, where he is busy restoring an old house, writing poems, and sculpting.

Bill Nevins' poems (115, 164) have appeared in many anthologies and magazines. He has read at venues like the Maple Leaf (New Orleans), Bowery Poetry Café (NYC), and Taos Poetry Circus. His collection *Heartbreak Ridge* was published in 2014 by Swimming with Elephants. He is featured in the 2007 documentary *Committing Poetry in Times of War.* He lives in Albuquerque.

Loren Niemi (168) is an innovative storyteller, author of a poetry chapbook, *Coyote Flies Coach* (Sister Black Press) and *The New Book of Plots* (on the uses of narrative in storytelling and fiction), and co-author with Elizabeth Ellis of the critically acclaimed, *Inviting the Wolf In: Thinking About Difficult Stories.*

David Michael Nixon (4, 14) has had four poetry chapbooks and one full-length, limited-edition poetry book published. His poems have appeared in many magazines and anthologies. *Stephen Forgives the Stones: New and Selected Poems* will be out from FootHills Publishing in Summer, 2018. He is also an a cappella singer.

Maril Nowak (40, 136) lives in the middle of New York State, the middle of nowhere, trying to imagine the middle, left, and right of Somewhere Else who voted for The Bloviator. She takes great comfort in Mencken's words. Americans survived Warren Harding, the original bloviator; we will survive this one too.

Jules Nyquist (vii, 179) is the founder of Jules' Poetry Playhouse, a place for poetry and play in Albuquerque where Jules teaches poetry classes and hosts visiting writers. She took her MFA from Bennington College. Jules' poems have appeared in *5 AM, Salamander, Malpais Review, Adobe Walls, A View from the Loft, Gray Sparrow, House Organ, Duke City Fix, Café Review* and others. Her website is www.julesnyquist.com

Mark W. Ó Brien (82) has been widely published at home and abroad. Is an alumnus of the 2014 Fermoy International Poetry Festival in Fermoy, County Cork. He has published three poetry collections: *Neo-Lethean Dreams* (2009), *Telluric Voices* (2013), *Lenticular Memories* (2014).

Mary Oertel-Kirschner (78) is an Albuquerque poet and painter. In her previous wage-earning life, she worked as a journalist and publicist. Her poems capture life experiences and insights that she wants to hold fast, and she hopes they produce a "ping" of connection for readers.

Chad Parenteau (60) is the current host and organizer of the Stone Soup Poetry series in Cambridge Massachusetts. His first full-length poetry collection, *Patron Emeritus,* was published by FootHills Publishing in 2013. He serves as Associate Editor of the online journal *Oddball Magazine.*

Michael Peters (194) is the author of *Vaast Bin* and other assorted language art works. As certain as he is uncertain of access to "the real," Peters frequently probes this periphery in a variety of old and new media, utilizing sound-imaging strategies as something like a poet, a visual poet, a fictioneer, an essayist, an ecologist, a musician, and a programmer.

Margaret Plaganis' (5) collage-poetry-books, "*Untitled*", "*Learning to Spell and Other Things*" and *"Uncharted Waters"* are in The Brooklyn Art Library Collection: https://www.sketchbookproject.com/libraries. Collaborations with Very Special Arts Connecticut and Yale School of Medicine led her to teach visual arts and special education in Hartford Public Schools.

Colleen Powderly's (147, 218) early poems reflecting her childhood in the Deep South and years spent in the Midwest form the basis for her book Split, published by FootHills Publishing (2009). Recent work focuses on stories from the working class, particularly from women's lives. She lives in Rochester NY. She keeps writing poems because she simply cannot stop.

Declan Quinn (124, 130) is from a rural village just outside Derry in Northern Ireland, and has been writing poetry and stories for a number of years. He says, "Only about 3 years ago I crashed hard and my mental health took a poor turn that I began to write earnestly. It is Catharsis at its finest for me and I hope my poems resonate with fellow Warriors."

Sylvia Ramos Cruz (2, 183) writes poems eclectic in form and content, inspired by works of art in all their forms, women's lives, and everyday injustices. Her award-winning work appears in local and national publications. She is a retired general surgeon and breast surgeon, avid gardener, and fully engaged women's rights activist.

Margaret Randall's (44, 135) most recent book of poems is *The Morning After: Poetry & Prose in a Post-Truth World* (Wings Press 2017). Duke University Press published her bilingual anthology of eight decades of Cuban poetry, *Only the Road/Solo el camino* (2016) and *Exporting Revolution: Cuba's Global Solidarity* (2017). Wings Press is bringing out her *Times Language: Selected Poems 1959-2018*, celebrating 60 years of poetry published in 30 collections, which she will launch on September 18, 2018 at City Lights Books in San Francisco.

John Roche (12, 88, 106, 184, 200) is the author of *On Conesus, Topicalities, Road Ghosts, and The Joe Poems: The Continuing Saga of Joe the Poet*, as well as the author of *Mo' Joe: The Anthology*. He believes we are going to need poetry to get through the next four years or forty years.

Charles Rossiter (16), NEA Fellowship Recipient, hosts the twice-monthly podcast series at www.PoetrySpokenHere.com. Recent books include *Winter Poems, Lakeside Poems*, and the latest, *Green Mountain Meditations*. He lives in Bennington VT, where he hosts the 2nd Tuesday open mic at the Tap House.

Janet Ruth (154, 196) is an emeritus research ornithologist from Corrales, NM. She has published scientific papers on bird ecology and natural history essays, as well as poems in *Grey Sparrow Journal, Value: Essays, Stories & Poems by Women of a Certain Age*, and *Santa Fe Literary Review*. Her new book, *Feathered Dreams: Celebrating Birds in Poems, Stories & Images*, is available from Mercury HeartLink Press.

Jane Sadowsky's work (11) has appeared in *Beyond Bones, The Empty Chair, Voices from the Herd, The Still Empty Chair, Earth's Daughters, Mo' Joe, Birdsong, The Sexuality Poems, A Celebration of Western New York Poets*, and the *Buffalo News*. She never suspected the greatest threat to our survival would come from within.

Ed Sanders (177) recently published a long Investigative Poem called *Broken Glory, The Final Years of Robert Kennedy*, illustrated by Rick Veitch (Arcade Publishers). He lives in Woodstock with his wife, Miriam, a painter and essayist.

Georgia Santa Maria (95, 214) is a Native New Mexican who has been an artist and writer most of her life. In 2012 she was a Guest Editor for LUMMOX Poetry Anthology, Issue I. Her book of poetry and photographs, *Lichen Kisses*, was published in 2013, and her book *Dowsing* is just out. She was first runner-up for the LUMMOX 5 Poetry Prize.

Marc Schillace's (105) love of learning has taken him from the study of art and eastern philosophy at Rhode Island School of Design to Oxford University where he read in Shakespearean Sonnets and philosophical anthropology. He finds writing poetry to be the most satisfying way to express his feelings and develop his ideas about experience and the meaning of existence.

Larry Schulte (117) is a visual artist who plays with words. He has been writing poetry for a few years, and has studied with poets Hermine Meinhard in NYC, and Michelle Brooks and Diane Thiel at the University of New Mexico.

Gretchen Schulz (32, 142, 162) is an Activist Artist at Large.

Elaine G. Schwartz (148) is a wife, mother, grandmother, retired college instructor, social activist and co-founder of the Albuquerque Chapter of Poets Against War. Her work has appeared in numerous publications including the *Santa Fe Literary Review*, *Malpais Review*, and *Sin Fronteras*.

G. E. Schwartz (79, 133), author of *Only Others Are: Poems* (Legible Press), *World (*Furniture Press), *Odd Fish* (Argotist), and *Thinking in Tongues* (Hank's Loose Gravel Press), was born in Pottsville, Pennsylvania in 1958.

Patricia Roth Schwartz (50, 166) is a poet and writer from New York's Finger Lakes. Widely published in small press journals, she has seven books of poems, including *Charleston Girls, a Memoir in Poems of a West Virginia Childhood*, and *The Crows of Copper John, a History of Auburn Prison in Poems*. From 2001 to 2015, she facilitated an inmates' poetry workshop inside Auburn Correctional Facility in Auburn, NY; her memoir of this experience, *Soul Knows No Bars,* will be out in Fall of 2018 from Olive Trees.

Mari Simbaña (56, 58) was born in Quito, Ecuador and grew up in Albuquerque, New Mexico. Within the areas of migration, local communities, and quotidian life, her work explores such themes as resilience, belonging, and love. Mari holds a B.A. in International Relations from Mt. Holyoke College and an M.A. in Community and Regional Planning from the University of New Mexico.

Danielle Taana Smith (59) is a professor of African American Studies at Syracuse University. Her essays, articles and poetry have appeared in various scholarly and literary journals. She is the co-editor of *Cultures of Fear: A Critical Reader*, an interdisciplinary volume with essays by leading scholars that investigate the everyday regimes of fear in a global context.

Jared Smith (81, 189): His 13th volume of poetry, *Shadows Within the Roaring Fork*, is available from Flowstone Press in Oregon. He is Poetry Editor of *Turtle Island Quarterly* and he now resides in the foothills of The Rockies, right outside Boulder, Colorado. His website, with more information, is www.jaredsmith.info

Joseph Somoza (108) was born in Spain and grew up in New Jersey and Chicago. After a stint studying pre-med, he switched to English and began writing poetry. He taught English at NMSU and elsewhere, retiring in 1995. He's published ten books and chapbooks of poetry, most recently *As Far as I Know* (Cinco Puntos, 2015). He and wife Jill, a painter, have three children and six grandchildren.

Nathanael William Stolte (20) is the author of *A Beggar's Book of Poems, Bumblebee Petting Zoo, Fools' Song, Origami Creature, & A Beggar's Prayer Book*. His poems have appeared in *Ghost City Review, Guide to Kulture, Trailer Park Quarterly,* and *In Between Hangovers,* among others. He is Acquisitions Editor for CWP Collective Press. Stolte was voted best poet in Buffalo by *Artvoice* in 2016. He is a madcap, flower-punk, D.I.Y. Buffalo-bred & corn-fed poet.

When **Elise Stuart** (46) moved to New Mexico in 2005, her heart opened to the desert, and her writing was revived. She was Silver City's Poet Laureate from 2014-2017 and gave 100 workshops to youth. In 2017, she published two books: *Another Door Calls*, a collection of poetry, and *My Mother and I, We Talk Cat*, a memoir.

Robbie Sugg (161, 201) grew up in the San Francisco Bay Area. His poetry has appeared in journals including *Elohi Gadugi, Earthen Lamp* (India), *The Café Review, Cape Cod Poetry Review, The Newport Review,* and *Flying Fish*. His first book, *Koccha and Other Poems*, was published in 2014 by DaysEye Press. His artwork has been exhibited throughout the US and England. He currently resides in Albuquerque.

F. Richard Thomas (80) has ten collections of poetry, including *Frog Praises Night* (Southern Illinois University Press), *Death at Camp Pahoka* (Michigan State University Press), *Extravagant Kiss* (Sin Fronteras Press), and his latest book, *Once in a Liifetime* (Years Press). His fiction includes the novella *Prism: The Journal of John Fish* (Canoe Press).

Steve Tills (169) publishes theenk Books in Palmyra, NY. His own books include *Invisible Diction* (Loose Gravel, Arroyo Grande, 1996); *Mr. Magoo* (Hank's Original, 1997); *Behave* (D-PRESS, 2004); a chapbook from *Helen Keller Series* (PO25centEM, 2004); *Rugh Stuff* (theenk Books, 2009), *Post Maiden* (Hank's Original, 2012). He has four+ books forthcoming (*Life Sentences Vol. 1, 2008-2016*; *The Collected Poems of Frank Stetson, Translated by Agnes Borgnine*; *The Helen Keller Series*; and *Life Sentences 2018*).

Martha Treichler (221) is a retired teacher and a retired Registered Dietitian. She lives on a farm on a hill near Hammondsport, NY. During the 1948-49 school year, she studied with Charles Olson at Black Mountain College. Martha has published five books of poems with FootHills Publishing.

Roslye Ultan (110) draws on her visual background and interest in nature to write poetry on the wonders of everyday life. She fills a white page with color, form, and the rhythm of existence. Ultan is Senior Faculty at the University of Minnesota/College of Continuing Education, and has curated exhibitions on the intersection of the arts and environment at the Institute on the Environment.

Richard Vargas (10) earned his BA at Cal State, Long Beach, where he studied under Gerald Locklin, and holds an MFA from U. New Mexico. He edited/published *The Tequila Review*, 1978-1980, and *Más Tequila Review*, 2010-2015. His first book, *McLife*, was featured on the Writer's Almanac in 2006. *American Jesus* was published by Tia Chucha Press (2007) and *Guernica, revisited* by Press 53 (2014). Currently, he resides in Rockford, IL, where he would give his left testicle for a green-chile-and-bacon breakfast burrito.

Stewart S. Warren (86, 198), author of over 20 poetry collections, is a drifter and evocateur whose work is both personal and transpersonal with a mystic undercurrent. Stewart is the owner of Mercury HeartLink, an independent New Mexico press for discriminating writers that supports them in realizing their artistic visions.

Denise Weaver Ross (cover, 3, 7) is an artist, poet and graphic designer who lives and works in Albuquerque. Her images are richly layered with cultural, political, and historical references. Denise graduated from UMass–Amherst with an MFA, regularly exhibits in the Southwest, and contributes her design abilities to local writers, artists and galleries. Her art and poetry can be found in many local and international magazines and anthologies.

Lawrence Welsh (123) has published nine books of poetry, including *Begging for Vultures: New and Selected Poems, 1994-2009* (UNM Press). This collection won the New Mexico-Arizona Book Award. It was also named a Notable Book by Southwest Books of the Year and a finalist for both the PEN Southwest Book Award and Writers' League of Texas Book Award.

Fred Whitehead (173) is co-editor of the anthology, *Freethought on the American Frontier* (Prometheus, 1992), and co-editor of the anthology *Poetry of Resistance: A Co-operative Anthology* (John Brown Press, 2014), as well as editions of the poetry of Don Gordon and Vincent Ferrini from the University of Illinois Press.

Scott Wiggerman (19, 120) is the author of three books of poetry, most recently *Leaf and Beak: Sonnets*, finalist for the Texas Institute of Letters' Helen C. Smith Memorial Award; and the editor of a dozen books, including the best-selling *Wingbeats I & II: Exercises & Practice in Poetry* (Dos Gatos Press). Recent poems have appeared in *Softblow, The Ghazal Page*, and *Allegro Poetry Magazine*.

Dwain Wilder's (112, 186, 187) publications include *Under the Only Moon* and poems in *Kudzu Review, Shadow/Play, Le Mot Juste, Lake Affect, Hot Air and Zen Bow*. He is past editor of *Zen Bow*, and co-edited *Liberty's Vigil: The Occupy Anthology*, and Vig*il for the Marcellus Shale*. Dwain lives in a small cottage beside a large dark forest.

Pamela Williams (206) is a poet and visual artist, with a lifelong habit of artistic expression. After thirty expansive years in the San Francisco area, New Mexico's extreme contrasts and rich history are providing alchemical inspiration and empowerment, fueling her poetry/assemblages, her Etsy shop NextSegue, and her first collection of poetry, *Hair on Fire*, available at Amazon.com.

Martin Willitts, Jr. (107, 114) won the 2014 Dylan Thomas International Poetry Contest. He has over 20 chapbooks including the winner of the *Turtle Island Quarterly* Editor's Choice Award, *The Wire Fence Holding Back the World* (Flowstone Press, 2016), plus 11 full-length collections including *Dylan Thomas and the Writing Shed* (FutureCycle Press, 2017).

Holly Wilson (89) lives in Albuquerque, New Mexico, where she has been active in the poetry community for many years. She is one of the members of the Beatlick Sisters, a multimedia performance poetry duo. Politics is one of her favorite topics to talk and write about.

Linda Yen (140) is a retired poverty lawyer who writes poetry on the sly. She somehow managed to publish in a few small presses, such as *New York Quarterly*, *Pearl*, and *Half Tones to Jubilee*, and has received several awards for her poems."

Leah Zazulyer (195) writes poetry, translates Yiddish poetry, and was a special education teacher and school psychologist. She lives in Rochester, NY, but grew up in California in a bilingual family from Belarus. She has published 5 poetry books and 2 books of translations of Israel Emiot.

Beverly Zeimer (61) is a Southern Ohio writer whose award-winning chapbook Pick a Way (Pudding 2009) details the lives of farm families. She has been published in various journals and anthologies including A Community of Voices: Reflections on Identity and Diversity (the College of Wooster), and Every River on Earth: Writing from the Appalachian Ohio (Shawnee State University). She lives in the Darby Valley.

JULES POETRY PLAYHOUSE PUBLICATIONS
Jules Nyquist is the founder and operator of Jules' Poetry Playhouse in
Albuquerque, NM, a place for poetry and play
http://www.julesnyquist.com

&

BEATLICK PRESS

Writers with Something to Say
Beatlick Press was established in 2011 to honor the memory of
Beatlick Joe Speer of Albuquerque, New Mexico and continue his
artistic mission to publish deserving writers:

Pamela Adams Hirst, publisher
Beatlick Press
Albuquerque, NM
http://beatlick.com/

Made in the USA
San Bernardino, CA
16 July 2018